The *Essential* Fundraising Handbook for Small Nonprofits

Betsy Baker | Kirsten Bullock | Gayle L. Gifford | Pamela Grow
Lori L. Jacobwith | Marc A. Pitman | Sandy Rees | Sherry Truhlar

The Essential Fundraising Handbook

for

Small Nonprofits

The Essential Fundraising Handbook

for

Small Nonprofits

by Betsy Baker | Kirsten Bullock | Gayle L. Gifford |
Pamela Grow | Lori L. Jacobwith | Marc A. Pitman |
Sandy Rees | Sherry Truhlar

To all of the caring people working to raise funds for small nonprofits everywhere. Your dedication and commitment makes a difference in lives everywhere.

Thank you for all you do.

Contents

Chapter 1: Vision
By Sandy Rees, CFRE

Small Shop, *Big Vision*

No matter what size your organization is, having a clear and compelling vision helps people understand what you're trying to accomplish and helps draw them into your organization's family. But having a *big vision* is critical to your success as a small nonprofit. Your *big vision* becomes a rallying force and a magnet for attracting support.

Think for a moment about the March of Dimes. When this organization began, their mission was to eradicate polio. It was a *big vision*. They didn't just want to eliminate polio in the United States, but worldwide. And they accomplished it. It took some time and a lot of effort, but they wiped out polio (except for a few places on the planet where it's being addressed by Rotary International).

Look carefully at every organization you consider successful. I bet they each have a clear vision they are working to achieve. And it's something impressive. Maybe they're working to eliminate illiteracy in their community, or to find homes for every homeless person or animal.

About Sandy

I grew up in a family that did a lot to help others. Both my grandfathers were preachers, and my parents were the kind to help anyone, anywhere, anytime. Add to that the fact that my dad was very involved in the Jaycees, spearheading a lot of activities to benefit the community, and you can see the perfect storm that formed for me. I was destined to be a do-gooder!

In 1998, I received a newsletter from Knox Area Rescue Ministries, one of the local nonprofits I supported. Mixed in with the stories of the homeless they served was an invitation to call the organization to get more involved. So I did. And a few weeks later, I was asked to join their board. I was *so* excited to be able to help. Being a "board member" sounded wonderful and important (even though I had absolutely *no* idea what that meant!). About a year later, there was a need to add someone to the development staff; and oddly enough, what they needed matched my skill set. I was working in corporate marketing at the time, and fundraising looked like the same thing to me—only it was about selling a warm fuzzy instead of a product or service. I applied and the rest is history.

After a year at the rescue mission wrangling volunteers, managing events, and running the thrift store, I took the job of Director of Development for Second Harvest Food Bank. I was there for five years, and it was five of the most fun years of my life. I had the chance to learn and grow and try things out. I made mistakes and experienced huge successes. I learned what works and what doesn't in just about every area of fundraising.

From there, I spent a year at the Joy of Music School, raising money to provide music lessons for kids who otherwise wouldn't get them. The kids were fabulous, but I was starting to get the itch to do something different. I became disillusioned with working for folks who didn't see the big vision I could see for the organization. I had a couple of false starts before I started Sandy Rees Consulting in December of 2005. It's been a fun, wild ride—full of personal satisfaction at watching nonprofits experience fundraising success. My mission now is to help as many nonprofits as possible raise the money of their dreams.

Whatever their vision, it's something that people can easily imagine in their minds and understand the impact.

A *big vision* goes beyond your nonprofit's reason for existence. Your mission statement may express why your organization was created, but a *big vision* excites people with its big impact. I like to say "play big or go home!" If a nonprofit exists, it should have as big an impact as possible. After all, what's the point of working so hard if your organization isn't going to do something very worthwhile?

It doesn't matter what kind of services you offer; a *big vision* will help you stand out in the nonprofit crowd. Whether your organization is an animal shelter, food bank, after-school program, medical center, or any other kind of nonprofit, a *big vision* will help set you up as *the* organization in the community. Your nonprofit will be the one in town that's up to something special and attracts all the movers and shakers to serve on the board, chair committees, and support campaigns. Your *big vision* will make you different in the donors' minds as well. Instead of being just one among dozens of unremarkable nonprofits, you'll be the fresh, exciting one doing something that really matters.

Once you create a *big vision*, your commitment to it must be unwavering. No matter what happens, you must be committed to seeing it through. When you stay focused on the vision, you'll be more likely to stay on track and not get off into the ditch, chasing dollars to start programs that don't have anything to do with your mission.

Why You Need a *Big Vision*

There are lots of reasons why your small nonprofit needs a *big vision*.

A *big vision* attracts supporters. A *big vision* is very interesting to donors. After all, donors don't want to get on board with a group that is constantly apologizing for their lack of impact, or begging for assistance to get out of crisis mode, or blaming their leadership for their lack of success. People don't want to get involved with something that even remotely looks like a sinking ship! Instead, donors want to get on board with a group that is radiating success. They love being a part of a group that is passionately championing a cause and changing the status quo. People like helping make something magical and wonderful happen, especially when it has long-lasting impact.

Nonprofits with big dreams and the confidence to achieve them will draw more loyal and generous donors. When your *big vision* sets people's hearts on fire, they will give—and likely give big gifts—to help the vision become a reality.

A *big vision* creates the foundation for strategic and operational plans. One of my favorite stories is from *Alice in Wonderland* where Alice meets the Cheshire cat and asks him for help. "Where do you want to go?" the cat asks. "I don't much care," says Alice. "Then any road will get you there," responds the cat. It's the same thing with organizational planning. Without a vision to shine a light on the destination you want to reach, it's going to be tough to get there. You could wander aimlessly as an organization, dabbling in programs, helping a few people along the way, but never really having much of an impact. Your *big vision* will provide the destination so that you can create the road map to get there. It sets the stage for the plans that are needed to fulfill the vision.

Having a clear vision actually makes the planning process easy. When you know that you want to eliminate substandard housing, or that you want to make sure that no child goes to bed hungry, it helps you clearly define the programs you need in place to reach that vision. From there, you can figure out how many staff you need and what the programs will cost to run, giving you the ability to clearly articulate how much money you need to raise. There's no need to guess or to shoot for raising "as much as possible." By the way, successful organizations always start with the vision and planning first, then figure out how to raise the money, instead of raising as much as possible then deciding how to spend it. Don't let the tail wag the dog!

A *big vision* shifts you from being reactive to being proactive. When you know very clearly where your nonprofit is heading, and you create plans to get there, you know exactly what to do every day. Gone are the days when you spend your time putting out fires. A clear vision gives you a yardstick to measure your activities by. For example, if your *big vision* is to eliminate hunger in your community, then you can look at each item on your to-do list and ask yourself, "Does this get us closer to eliminating hunger?" If the answer is yes, you do the task. If not, mark it off your list because you don't need to spend your time on it.

What a *Big Vision* Is

A *big vision* is an overarching goal so bold and audacious that it stretches your nonprofit to work toward it and reach it. You may have to change the way you are doing some things to become more efficient or more effective. Your *big vision* should give you goose bumps when you talk about it with others. It may move you to tears. Its impact will be profound and significant in the community, and many lives will be changed.

Your *big vision* should be compelling. When you talk about it in the community, people should start asking lots of questions to better understand it (this usually indicates their interest in supporting it!). Your *big vision* should be easy to explain and easy to understand. You shouldn't have to work hard to describe what you're trying to do.

Most important, everyone in a leadership position in your organization—both staff and board—should participate in creating the vision and supporting it. If you are missing a consensus about your *big vision*, go back and try again. You don't want any negative individuals pulling everyone else down while you're working to achieve something of this importance.

Your vision should be so big that it motivates your staff in a way that nothing else ever has before. Everyone should understand how their job impacts the achievement of the vision. They should also be willing to do whatever it takes.

When I worked at the food bank, we measured our success in the amount of food we distributed each year. We saw modest increases each year, and we patted ourselves on the back for a job well done—until I heard about another food bank that had figured out a way to estimate the need in their community. When I calculated it for our area, I saw that we needed to triple the amount of food we were handling if we were going to completely meet the need in East Tennessee. I shared this with my coworkers and our board, and we all agreed to significantly raise the bar on what we were doing. We took our jobs way more seriously after that. In the development office, we studied best practices. We created systems to streamline operations. We recruited more volunteers to help. And we tripled our annual fundraising in just a couple of years. You better believe that three times the money goes a long way toward three times the food!

A *big vision* can challenge staff, board members, and volunteers to overcome any personal obstacles that might be in the way, like their fear of fundraising. I've seen organizations where a common vision was just what some board members needed to get over their fear of fundraising and opening doors that they had never been willing to open before. I've seen executive directors overcome their fear of rejection and not only learn to cultivate donors for major gifts, but get them! I'm convinced that this happened because the vision gave them something worth working toward.

When you have a *big vision*, it virtually eliminates "competition." There's no need to worry about what other nonprofits are doing when you're working toward something with deep and lasting impact. In fact, your *big vision* will cause people to see your organization differently, and you'll stand out in their mind from the sea of other boring nonprofits out there.

A *big vision* will require more support than you are currently getting from the community. You'll need more donors and more dollars from the donors you already have. You'll find that when every donor and dollar counts, you'll become more donor-focused in your fundraising, which will help you keep—and grow—the donors you have. There will be a place for supporters at all levels, from the $5 gift to the $500,000 gift. You'll get very good at thanking donors and building relationships.

Your *big vision* will impact the way you talk about your organization and will be evident in all communications, print materials, and your online presence. You'll be much more focused on the results you're working toward and less focused on your need.

Big Vision Evaluation Checklist

Use this checklist to determine if your nonprofit has a *big vision*.

Your Nonprofit's *Big Vision*: _____

_____

_____

_____

_____

_____

Check the box if your nonprofit's vision meets the description. The more honest you are, the better.

- ☐ Needed in the community (however you define community)
- ☐ Interesting to donors
- ☐ Results-oriented
- ☐ Bold
- ☐ Compelling
- ☐ Simple and easy to understand (no jargon)
- ☐ Measurable
- ☐ Attainable and realistic (even though it may take some time to reach it)
- ☐ Created by all organizational leaders (staff and board)
- ☐ Supported by all organizational leaders (staff and board)
- ☐ Motivational
- ☐ Supported by programs and daily activities

Sample *Big Vision*

Here are a couple of samples of a *big vision*.

> Asheville Humane Society is the only open-admission shelter in the county, the only one that can never—and will never—close its doors or say "we're full."

> Habitat for Humanity's vision: "A world where everyone has a decent place to live."

> New Hope Children's Advocacy Center: "Our vision is that all children are loved, protected, nurtured, and educated."

Case for Support

One of the best ways to communicate your *big vision* is to develop a case for support. The collection of reasons why someone would give to your organization is called your case for support. Usually, it's in writing in a document called a *case statement* that you can share with donors, prospects, and the community.

This doesn't have to be complicated! In fact, the simpler, the better.

A case statement is a concise document that clearly explains what need your organization seeks to meet, how you have met and/or plan to meet that need, and what you could achieve with additional resources. It should motivate the reader to take action (and support your work with a financial gift). It should contain the right mix of detail, passion, and inspiration in an easy-to-read format.

Your case statement should be prepared for your donors and prospects, so keep it focused on them and what they are interested in. Don't make the mistake of writing it so that only "insiders" can understand it. Use simple language that anyone would understand, not industry jargon and acronyms. As you write, think about one of your best donors, and write as if you were talking with her. It will help you keep the text light and conversational.

Be sure to include a sense of urgency as you describe your *big vision* in your case statement. Remind the reader of the pressing need and how you must deliver your services now. If you don't, your reader may not respond.

Your case statement will serve as the foundational piece for all other promotional documents, such as brochures, grants, and press releases. It details your organization's mission, vision, history, and reason for seeking funds. And you should review it at least once a year to make sure it's still relevant and accurate. It does not need to be a lengthy document, but it must cover the important pieces.

Here are some questions you want to answer in your case statement.

> Why would someone give?
> What is your organization trying to accomplish?
> What makes the organization special?
> What is the organization's fundraising goal?
> How will the organization evaluate its programs?
> What has the organization achieved to date?

Who else supports this organization?

What's your unit of service?

What's your cost per unit of service?

What does it cost you to run each program
(program description and program budget)?

What stories can you tell about people you've
served?

What stories best illustrate the work your
organization does?

Format for Creating Your Case Statement

Here's a quick guide for formatting your case statement:

1. **History.** Describe your organization and share a brief history of your organization. What makes you special?

2. **Challenge and ramifications.** What are the challenges/threats your organization faces? What will be the impact on the community and the population you serve if those challenges go unmet? Do you have any recent research or statistics to demonstrate the need you're addressing?

3. **Who are you and what do you do?** What is your mission/vision? How large is your organization, and how many people do you serve? What are your primary programs or areas of focus? How much is your organizational budget, and what are your major revenue streams?

4. **What results are you shooting for?** What results has your organization achieved so far? What are your future plans? What are you planning to increase?

5. **How much will it cost?** Why are you asking for money? What is the cost of the work you are doing? What does it cost you to provide one unit of service? If this is a particular campaign, how much are you trying to raise? How will the money be spent? How can people contact you to donate?

Writing the Case Statement

The actual writing is usually a little trickier than anything else. You want to keep your mind focused on your donor as you write. This will help you include only those things your donor will be interested in.

Here are some tips for creating a successful, compelling case statement:

- **Know your audience**. Put yourself in your donor's shoes, and think about the things he or she is interested in about your organization. Ask yourself, "As a donor, why would I support this nonprofit? And why now?"

- **Write for an audience of one.** Think about a specific donor and write to him or her. This will help you maintain your focus on your reader.

- **Be sure to answer "What will my gift accomplish?"** Donors want to know what you'll do with their money and how their gift will make a difference.

- **Use the word *you* frequently.** *You* pulls the reader in and makes her part of the story. It engages her and helps her see the role she can play in helping your organization change the world.

- **Include key statistics if they will support your explanation of the need.**

- **Write with passion.** If your reader isn't moved to give, your case statement won't do you any good.

- **Leave out the jargon and industry terms.** Make sure someone with no knowledge of your organization can understand what you've written.

- **Sell the sizzle, not the steak.** Be sure to focus on the benefits of your programs, and not the details of the programs. Talk about how people's lives will be changed or saved by participating in your program. Share how they will benefit. This is the stuff that people want to read!

Writing the text is only part of creating a good case statement. The other part is to make the document look interesting to the reader. In other words, design gives your words power. Be sure to use plenty of white space in your document. If the page is full of text, no one will want to read it because it looks like too much work. Photos, bullets, and other graphical elements can break up the text and give the reader's eyes a place to rest. Use short paragraphs, headings, and anything else that will increase the readability of your case statement.

Use the Simple Case Statement Template to create your case statement. You'll likely refer back to this document as you create other fundraising and marketing documents for your organization, so set aside some time to work on this, and give it your best effort.

You may want to create a case statement for your organization as a whole and then one for each program or project for which you plan to raise money. Each program might have slightly different reasons for someone to give. For example, an animal shelter might have four case statements: one for the organization as a whole, and then one statement each for their spay/neuter program, kibbles program (for donations of dog food), and community awareness/education program. One size does not fit all, and one case statement won't work for every program, every donor, and every situation.

What are the programs or projects in your organization that might need a case statement?

_____

_____

_____

_____

_____

_____

_____

Use the Simple Program/Project Summary Worksheet to gather information for each program or project case statement.

Simple Case Statement Template

Your case statement is a summary of the reasons for people to give. You should have a case statement for your organization and one for individual programs or projects.

Before you attempt to craft a case statement, you may find it helpful to collect a copy of each of your organization's materials, like previous case statements, brochures, annual reports, newsletters, direct mail letters, and grant proposals. Often, you can reuse some of the information instead of starting from scratch.

1. What is your organization's mission statement? (It needs to be short, concise, and compelling.) _____

   _____

   _____

   _____

2. What problem does your organization address? (Feed the hungry, help the sick, house homeless animals, protect the environment, etc.) _____

   _____

   _____

   _____

3. How many people are affected by this problem in the area you serve? _____

_____

_____

4. Briefly describe your organization's history (why and how you came into being and your major milestones/accomplishments). _____

_____

_____

_____

5. What success has your organization had in addressing the problem? _____

_____

_____

_____

6. What success stories can you tell about the people you've helped? _____

_____

_____

_____

_____

7. How is the organization uniquely positioned to successfully address this problem? _____

_____

_____

_____

_____

8. For what need are you raising money? _____

_____

9. What is the fundraising goal for this need? _____

_____

10. How will the donor's gift affect the need? _____

_____

_____

_____

_____

_____

11. What makes the need urgent? (Why should the donor give now?) _____

_____

_____

_____

Simple Program/Project Summary Worksheet

Program/project name: _____

Purpose of program/project: _____

_____

_____

_____

Population served by this program/project: _____

_____

_____

Number of people served monthly or annually by this
program/project: _____

_____

_____

History and accomplishments of this
program/project: _____

_____

_____

Program/project budget: _____

Reason(s) why someone should support this
program/project: _____

_____

_____

_____

Sample Case Statement Worksheet: Habitat for Humanity

1. What is your organization's mission statement? (It needs to be short, concise, and compelling.) <u>Habitat for Humanity is an ecumenical, Christian housing ministry that builds simple, decent, affordable, energy-efficient homes in partnership with low-income families who do not otherwise have access to adequate housing.</u>

2. What problem does your organization address? (Feed the hungry, help the sick, house homeless animals, protect the environment, etc.) <u>Our mission is to work in partnership with God and people everywhere, from all walks of life, to develop communities with people in need by building and renovating houses, so that every person can experience the joy of a safe place to live and be proud to call home.</u>

3. How many people are affected by this problem in the area you serve? <u>According to the latest census, nearly four thousand people or 10% of the population of our county live in poverty. From</u>

this, we estimate that one thousand families live in substandard housing in our community. We also know that more than 850 households pay more than 35% of their income on rent, which doesn't leave enough to cover all the other living expenses.

4. Briefly describe your organization's history. Chartered in 1992, Habitat was formed by a group of concerned citizens who wanted to provide better housing for their neighbors. Since that time, the organization has grown from a group of volunteers to a staff of thirteen, including administrative, home store, and construction staff. Today, we're one of the leading real estate developers in our area, and we're known for our "green" building processes.

5. What success has your organization had in addressing the problem? Since 1982, we have built or improved ninety homes with no foreclosures. Most of those homes have been built from the ground up, adding dozens of families to the community's base of property taxpayers.

6. What success stories can you tell about the people you've helped? <u>In the past year, we had our first homeowner send a child to college. The mom told us she didn't think it would have happened without her house, because it provided the child with a bedroom of his own—a quiet place to study.</u>

7. How is the organization uniquely positioned to successfully address this problem?
<u>Through volunteer labor, effective management, and tax-deductible donations of money, materials, and services, Habitat builds more homes in our community than any commercial builder. And because of our careful screening process, we have never had to foreclose on a homeowner.</u>

8. For what need are you raising money? <u>Hope Haven is our newest project. It will be an environmentally friendly, planned neighborhood of Habitat families, situated on eighteen acres on Roberts Road. It's ideally located across the street from the elementary and middle schools. Our plan is to develop the land into a subdivision of sixty homes with development taking place in phases.</u>

Money is needed to develop the land and put in infrastructure (water, sewer, streets, sidewalks, etc.).

9. What is the fundraising goal for this need? We anticipate it will cost $1.2 million to install all the infrastructure elements.

10. How will the donor's gift affect the need? Every dollar will get us closer to getting the first phase build-ready. Once all the infrastructure is in place for phase 1, we can begin building houses on the lots.

11. What makes the need urgent? (Why should the donor give now?) As soon as we raise the money for phase 1, we will start on the infrastructure so we can get families into a home of their own as soon as possible.

Chapter 2: Board
By Gayle L. Gifford, ACFRE

As a small shop fundraiser, one of your most precious needs is mustering the help you need to raise money for your organization. So where can you turn?

Let me guess that your wishful eyes have turned toward your board of directors.

If you've been hanging out with any charity folks, you've probably developed the belief that your board members are "obligated" to be involved in fundraising. The mantra goes something like this: "It's the board's job to fundraise."

To that I say, *nonsense!*

I'm not rejecting the idea that board members might be important allies in fundraising. I am warning that you won't be successful in fundraising if you carry the idea that your board members are somehow "required" to fundraise just because they joined the board—and that all you have to do is have someone tell them they have to raise money.

And to be successful in fundraising is what you want to be, right?

About Gayle

I learned the power of fundraising for social change as a volunteer activist working for peace, human rights, and nuclear disarmament. A federal bureaucrat by day, in my free time I learned how to organize from amazing mentors who taught me to write press releases, speak in public, produce newsletters, and raise money through events like spaghetti suppers, direct mail, and personal asks.

Amazingly, my volunteer work landed me my first professional job in fundraising at the child sponsorship organization Foster Parents Plan (now PLAN USA). As Director of Development and Communications, I learned from some of the top direct marketers in the world. I left PLAN after my twins were born to work at more community-based organizations and honed my skills in corporate and foundation grant seeking, board and organization development.

Today, I advise nonprofits in governance, strategic planning, and fundraising as president of Cause & Effect Inc. I earned my CFRE in 1996 and my ACFRE in 2002, one of just one hundred fundraisers today who hold this advanced fundraising credential. I blog, teach, speak, and write. I'm the author of *How to Make Your Board Dramatically More Effective, Starting Today* and a contributor to books from the *Charity Channel* community. I earned a masters degree in organization and management from Antioch University–New England.

I serve on the board of WaterFire Providence and Blackstone Academy Charter High School and on the advisory councils of Latino Dollars for Scholars of RI and RI Museum of Science and Art. I live in Providence, RI, where I work with my fabulous husband. I'm a proud mom of three children.

For now, put that notion of board obligation out of your mind. Instead, think more strategically about how you can unleash the potential fundraising power of your board member volunteers—and increase your success in raising money for your nonprofit.

The Top Two Things Fundraisers Need Board Members to Be

There are two things that I think every fundraiser absolutely needs their board members to be.

Here's number 1 on my list:

1.   Board members are *courageous leaders* who ensure your organization is *the best* it can possibly be.

Have you ever tried to sell a mediocre product? It would be hard to be passionate about doing that, wouldn't it?

Or imagine if you talked someone into buying a poor-quality product. It's unlikely that person would buy from you a second time.

The same is true in fundraising. There is no ingredient more essential to fundraising success than being a high-quality organization that people want to donate to again and again.

What makes an organization giving-worthy?

- Doing something that really matters to people (hopefully to lots of people).
- Doing it really well.
- Having a significant impact on a problem or people or, as Sandy mentioned in the previous chapter, community.
- Verifying the impact you say you are having.
- Using the resources you've received responsibly and in the manner they were intended.
- Having amazing people work there.
- Treating people well—whether they are consumers, staff, volunteers, donors, or anyone else in your orbit.
- Walking the talk by living up to your values.
- Knowing where you are going and how others can contribute to your success.

This is a pretty important list.

And guess what? It aligns completely with the primary role of your board of directors.

Of course, in many nonprofits, it's the staff and, frequently, direct service volunteers who actually carry out the work of the organization.

But whether your organization has staff or not, at the end of the day, the people who serve in a governing role in your organization are the ones responsible for ensuring that the above list comes to life.

And those governors are your board of directors.

(A growing number of nonprofits are exploring ways to distribute governing functions beyond the traditionally organized board of directors. But that's for a different book.)

So how does the board ensure a giving-worthy organization?

The board of directors has to ask and answer many big questions. Among these are questions like:

- What does our community need?
- How exactly will we make our community better?
- What are we promising we will accomplish?
- What is the best way to get there?

- What kind of investment do we need to make to achieve our desired results?
- How will we pay for this?

The board hires a great executive director as a partner to think through those questions. The executive director also manages the work, along with other amazing staff who execute great programs.

The board has other jobs too. One is defining operational and financial health for the present and for the future. The board also has to attend to its own functioning by recruiting and training top-notch board members, working thoughtfully and responsibly, and observing its own operating rules and values. Ultimately, the board is responsible for holding everyone accountable, itself included, for excellence in the tasks they have taken on.

Throw onto all of this a heaping tablespoon of the legal responsibility for your organization's future, and wow! Being a board member is a really big job!

Yes, fundraisers would like our board members to put our needs first. In reality, the job of governing always comes out on top. A wise fundraiser never underestimates how much energy, training, and involvement it will take to help board members perform these basic governing functions really well. Really wise fundraisers are active in helping their boss and boards be as good at their governing tasks as they can possibly be. They pass along feedback gleaned from donors and others. They advocate for the things they need like strategic and business plans, multiyear budget forecasts, and research data.

Your life as a fundraiser will be forever easier with this solidly giving-worthy organization behind you—and a total struggle without it.

Now on to the second thing I believe all board members should be:

2. Board members are passionate cheerleaders who promote your organization with every contact they make.

As I said at the beginning, as a small shop fundraiser, you'll need all the (good) help you can get to accomplish the hard work of fundraising. For example, you'll need help:

- getting the word out to as many people as possible about the good work of your organization;
- making lots of connections that lead to new friends and future supporters;

- acquiring resources—whether that's information, expertise, money, people, partnerships, products, services, or influence; and
- thanking and recognizing your supporters.

In the end, raising money requires sifting through the huge universe of potential supporters to find the handful of people (relatively speaking) who, with the right information and excitement, would be interested in giving to your cause. And keeping them excited so they'll give again and again.

Because there are so many people to get to know, and a limited amount of your time, wouldn't it be nice to have qualified help to keep connected with all of your donors and prospective donors?

Your board members—given their numbers, their insider knowledge about your organization, their legal commitment to your success, and their community connections—have the potential to be extraordinary helpmates to any fundraiser.

When I'm recruiting board members, they always ask, "How much time is expected of me?" I tell them there are two answers to that question.

The first is the official time they'll put in at board and committee meetings and carrying out other assignments they may have.

The second is the unofficial time I also want from them. As they move through the day and encounter neighbors, friends, colleagues, or new acquaintances, I want them to always think and talk about our organization and introduce us to many new friends. Some board members may be naturals at this. Others are going to need lots of help. (Read on.)

Here's what you can never, ever do. Never just assume that it's your board's job to fundraise and expect your board members to spontaneously rise up to do it. Instead, let's take a clear-eyed look at what it takes to get board members involved in fundraising.

What It Takes to Turn Board Members into Fundraising Allies

Start by looking within.

Think about what it took to develop yourself into a fundraiser.

Few of us were born into this world—ready to ask other people for money. Just look at the stories of the coauthors of this book. Like them, many fundraisers I know landed in this career from another profession or because of a volunteer assignment.

How did you start?

Maybe you were lucky to be a development associate, where you learned on the job to manage a donor database or some event logistics or to prepare thank-you letters, among other tasks. As an associate, you heard the stories and carefully watched how your development director or other fundraisers performed their jobs.

Or maybe you drifted into fundraising from programs, marketing, communications, special events, or even from business. Perhaps you started as a grant writer and had the opportunity to learn how to put together a good case for support and to ask questions of program officers.

If you were lucky, you've been to conferences and workshops or read books and articles on many different aspects of fundraising. Perhaps you've been taken under the wing of experienced fundraisers who have shown you the way.

Or maybe you are just starting out as a small shop fundraiser and are only now learning all of this on your own.

Regardless of how you started, when you tap into your own memories, you'll likely remember your own fears about fundraising and what it took to conquer those fears. Many longtime fundraisers still confess that they need to psych themselves up each time they get around to saying the words, "Would you consider a gift of _____?"

Now think about your board members and their background in fundraising.

If you are lucky, some of your board members have had pleasant experiences raising money. Maybe they successfully sold tickets for an event. If you are really, really lucky, one or two actually enjoy or have experience asking other people for money.

But if your board is like most others, the majority of your board members are still in the fear stage, worrying "do I really have to ask people for money?" Few have had any of your experience or training in fundraising.

Now we all know that there are many fundraising tasks that don't involve asking for money—like thanking the donors we have. But whenever you say the word *fundraising* to a board member, all he hears is that you are asking him to ask someone else for money.

To help board members get over their fear of participating in any aspect of fundraising, never underestimate the amount of training and carefully crafted successful experiences you'll need to create for your reluctant volunteers. I'll talk more about how to do that in a minute.

Remember, you are the professional.

You were hired to be the fundraiser for your organization. Your board members were recruited to be governors first and foremost. It is your job to fundraise.

As a consultant, I can't tell you the number of times I've heard executive directors or directors of development blame their lack of fundraising success on their board. "I wasn't able to raise money because my board won't fundraise." Or "We have the wrong board members to be successful."

When I probe more deeply, these individuals bought into the idea that "it's the board's job to fundraise." They think that this will happen on its own and without significant enabling from staff.

These expectations are fueled by the infrequent examples of nonprofits that have successful board participation in fundraising. Yet the storyteller usually forgets to share the details—the details where staff spend quite a lot of time supporting those board members in their efforts.

I always say that staff who rely on their volunteer board members for significant parts of their budget, without managing that process from soup to nuts, are likely to end up unemployed when the money doesn't arrive.

Sure, it may not be easy for a mere development director to get through the door to all the donors you need. It isn't easy for big institution fundraisers either. You need to be creative and persistent. Having board members with connections can be a very big help—but only if they are willing to use them.

It's up to you to have a plan for exactly how your board members can help.

In my years of experience as a fundraiser, a board member, and a consultant, I've learned that board members really don't know what to do.

They are expecting you to provide them with guidance. They want you to hold their hand all along the way.

To do that, you've got to know what you need and how best to use your volunteer board members.

It all starts with your development plan. How exactly are you going to raise the money you need to raise? Do the math. Among the goals and strategies, the activities and the calculations, you'll be able to identify exactly where you need additional people power to get the job done.

Instead of "expecting" your board members to fill those jobs, try thinking of them as just some of the many volunteers you might recruit to assist you in fundraising. You have other potential volunteers too—buried within your current donor list, among former board members, and even people you haven't met yet. And then you'll want to match the right people to the right task.

Because there are so many different aspects to fund development, you won't lack for assignments. I'm sure you can find a job that even the most reluctant board member would be willing to help you with.

Here's a starting list of things that you might need help doing:

- Getting to know your current donors by sitting down with them over a cup of coffee.

- Engaging your current donors in activities in your organization that they might enjoy and learn from.
- Asking your current donors for an investment in your organization.
- Thanking your current donors.
- Keeping your donors informed about your organization's good work.
- Keeping an eye out for things that happen to your donors in their own lives.
- Finding prospective, new donors.
- Meeting those prospective, new donors.
- Strategizing approaches to current and prospective donors.
- Recruiting goods or services for your programs.
- Recruiting goods or services for your events.
- Finding lower-cost but high-quality vendors.

But here's where it gets tricky. You can't assign fundraising goals to people who haven't signed up for the job.

Match the right person with the right job.

After thinking about what jobs need doing, think about what skills and qualifications are needed in the people you will recruit to fill those jobs.

To do the best matching you can, personally interview each board member. You'll learn a whole lot this way— why they joined this board, why they care about your organization, what talents they might want to contribute, what they hope to accomplish in their board service, their level of passion and commitment, and what volunteer work they are already doing. You can also take this opportunity to talk about their giving, but more on that a little later. Probe for what types of fundraising experiences they have had. Also find out what type of help they might need to get involved. Share your specific cultivation, solicitation, and stewardship activities with them, and see where they feel comfortable participating.

- Many can be door openers and help make connections.
- A few will be fabulous strategists.
- A few will be passionate and tireless advocates for the mission and program approach.
- Others couldn't be better at writing thank-you notes or hosting thank-you events.
- Some will even be willing to help ask for money.

Just like any other job, not every person comes equipped with all the competencies, skills, and desires to fill every position. Some board members will already have had some experience. Others will have the inclination to help but need training and ongoing guidance.

I can pretty much guarantee that there will be a few board members you'll scratch from your list for now. They simply aren't interested (yet) and will resist your efforts to engage them. That's okay. *Don't be angry; don't resent their unwillingness; work with what you've got.*

Start with the willing few.

Let's be real. Fundraising is not a volunteer job that people jump onto a board with the skills for success. They may not necessarily want to participate at all. (Sure, sure, every board member can help thank donors, but will everyone?)

If you're really lucky, you might have one or two individuals who come totally prepared—with the skills and commitment—to fill your toughest job slot of volunteer solicitor. You may even have a few individuals who are game to try it if you provide them with lots of personal support.

But most likely, you've got a big group of solicitation-terrified board members who bring lots of other critical knowledge to your nonprofit and may even be working incredibly hard in other volunteer roles (beyond the hard work they do as governors).

So if you, the development professional whose job it is to raise funds, need some board members to assist, you are going to have to work very, very hard, one-on-one, to help them be successful.

As a small shop fundraiser, this is time-consuming work. So make very sure that this is the work that you need to do. You might find that your time is much better spent working directly with donors than trying to turn reluctant board members into fundraisers.

I recently discovered that many good fundraisers have felt for years that they were somehow failing because they couldn't get 100% of their board members to participate in fundraising (not giving, but fundraising). One experienced development director told me that even though she had a half-dozen board members she could count on to support fundraising, she still didn't feel that she was succeeding.

Why, even the guru of fundraising Jerold Panas says, *"If you have three to four really great fundraising volunteers, you are luckier than most development officers! You will be successful."*

So start with a few—beginning with the ones who are ready and willing to step out of their comfort zone. And congratulate yourself on the successful progress you have made.

Turning board members into donors.

One of the axioms of fundraising is that before you can ask someone else for money, you need to make your own gift first.

This is true with our board members as well. Every board would be happy with 100% giving from its members.

What makes fundraisers really happy is when board members willingly stretch to give as generously as they can for their financial circumstances. This happens when they are emotionally invested, personally excited, meaningfully engaged, and thoroughly convinced that their gifts and your organization make an important difference.

Guess what? Getting your board members to that point is also your job.

You'll need to craft a donor cultivation plan for each of your board members, whether they participate in fundraising activities or not.

At the heart of your success will be creating an amazing, memorable experience(s) for each one of your board members—the one that transforms them from dutiful givers to true believers.

For some organizations, that's a life-changing trip to a foreign land or a local neighborhood to witness firsthand the great need and uplifting resilience. Or it's that tour of the neonatal intensive care unit informed by the voices of nurses and parents sharing their own heart-touching experiences of love and survival.

No matter your cause, there are always experiences that you can develop that will forever touch the hearts of your board members. It might be rolling up their sleeves as a direct service volunteer in your program. Or seeing or talking to the people who benefit from the work you do.

And you'll be doing double duty as these experiences you are creating for board members will probably be the same experiences that you offer to other donors as well.

Some board members will experience that transformation because you asked them the questions that enabled them to tap deeply into their own dreams for the future. And then matched them with opportunities to fulfill those dreams. Questions like:

- What brought you to care about this issue?
- What injustice makes your blood boil, or what cause gets you fired up?
- What giving has made you feel great?
- What do you want to be your legacy?
- How will the world be different because of your giving?

These experiences are designed to help answer the question that fundraiser Alan Sharpe, CFRE of the Harvey McKinnon Groups, says every fundraiser must answer: *How will my donation change the world?*

Of course, you've got to make the specific case for how your board members' donations will make a difference.

It also goes without saying that someone will have to ask each board member for their donation. That might be you. But often it will be (with your support) your board president, executive director, or maybe the chair of your board fundraising campaign who will make the ask. This circles right back into our discussion of how to turn your board members into fundraisers.

View yourself as a people mobilizer.

Like any good supervisor, manage your volunteer team for
success:

- Create bite-sized tasks that volunteers can
  successfully accomplish.
- Offer a menu of options.
- Match the right person to the job.
- Be very clear about the goal, and put it in writing.
- Cowrite agreements with each of your board
  volunteers that outline their commitments—
  including what will be accomplished, by when, and
  what support and feedback you'll provide.
- Live up to your own obligations.
- Give your volunteers ongoing feedback.
- Help them solve problems.
- Celebrate important milestones.

Always remember that your board members are
volunteers—no matter how passionate they are about
your nonprofit, they've got other jobs and responsibilities,
which will always command their first loyalties.

So be patient. Follow up, follow up, follow up on
assignments.

Is a member "forgetting" to make their phone calls? Make sure they have a script. Practice it. Then schedule a meeting for them to make those calls with you standing by their side.

Do you have board members willing to write personal notes on your annual appeal? How about a wine and cheese gathering or breakfast where you provide the refreshments, letters, pens, and even starting ideas for the content of the notes?

Remember that few people can put something new into practice just by hearing it described. Many need to watch someone else do it before they try it the first time. Let your board members know that they won't have to do anything alone until they and you feel they are ready.

Say "thank you"—a lot! Handwritten notes are always appreciated (and don't cost very much).

Because none of us can do everything, remember to invest your greatest energy in the tasks and volunteers who will make the most difference. Don't waste time trying to move unmovable objects or doing the same ineffective thing over and over.

A friend of mine used to say, "No one notices when you dust the corners." That is, don't waste your time meeting an unrealistic definition of perfection; keep moving with what you've got instead of fretting about what you don't have.

Should you have a board fund development committee?

You will hear from many of your colleagues that you have to have a fund development committee to get board members involved in fundraising.

I'd like to suggest that you think carefully about your needs before you jump into creating the typical all-purpose fund development committee.

As you've learned above, the successful fundraising partnerships you'll create with board members will most likely happen one-on-one and not in a group setting.

After years of serving as a development director and as a fundraising consultant, here are a few of the challenges my colleagues and I have encountered that come with such a wide-ranging committee.

- Few voluntarily want to serve on it.
- Those who do had their arms twisted and are reluctantly serving.
- When you suggest a strategy that you know will work but sounds scary, the group supports one other in blocking the implementation of a task they find unpleasant.
- So many different fundraising jobs are heaped onto the same committee—policy making, special events, annual giving, large gifts, etc.—that people who were recruited because they were eager to work on one program get distracted by the other activities.

Again, as a small shop fundraiser, you'll need to be very protective of your time and use it very wisely when it comes to committees.

If you need leadership volunteers to support you in fundraising, then the most effective action you can take will be working with board members one-on-one on a specific objective.

But there might be projects where it does help to have committees or specific task forces. For example, you might need a committee to help you put on that special event. Or the camaraderie and encouragement of a committee could work for your large giver or corporate-giving campaigns. A more formal fund development committee might meet once or twice a year to review fundraising policy and to vet the fund development plan you recommend to the board.

Recruit each volunteer (whether a board member or not) for his/her skills and competencies to accomplish the task at hand. Give each person a specific job to do or goal to reach that they have agreed to. Make sure everyone on the team knows any limitations or constraints on raising that money (e.g., when to check in before approaching a prospect or the budget limits on that special event).

In this approach, there is no ambiguity about the job of the volunteer or role of the committee. The job is to raise money following the plan outlined by the development staff and in alignment with the strategic direction approved by the board.

While volunteer advice is important to successful teamwork and to strategize the best way to approach a particular donor, it's clear to all that volunteers weren't recruited to "supervise" professional staff or to undo carefully forged development plans.

A fundraiser's checklist for working with board members:

1. *Appreciate them as givers or getters.* Remember, these volunteers still want and need to be appreciated, supported, cultivated, recognized, and celebrated—all the things you do for other donors and volunteers. Find out what each board member cares about, what motivates them, what they are willing or not willing to do.

2. *Don't use group decisions or the job description only to motivate individual action.* Group agreements are unreliable predictors of individual action. Nodding yes is easier than sharing what scares you or saying NO. And just because a commitment is on paper doesn't mean it's a go. That's why working one-on-one with your board members is the best way to prepare them for action.

3. *Encourage (never scold) to produce action.* It's tempting to want to "bring in the consultant to tell board members what they have to do." Now really, did that lecture work the first time? Personally, I'm not a fan of public shaming. And today's brain science validates that it's better to focus on and encourage more of what is working than to stay stuck on the negative.

4. *Don't assume; instead, create high levels of commitment or understanding of your mission.* Unfortunately, not every nominating process produces passionate advocates. Even true believers may not have enough understanding to confidently talk about your work. Try the personal action plan of personal experiences to raise the commitment of each board member (see number 9 below).

5. *Make sure board members really understand and are committed to the case for support.* Too many of us have insufficiently compelling cases for giving. Board members want to feel confident—especially when asking for operating funds (aka annual giving). It's so much easier to ask when you understand how outcomes and the money line up.

6. *Avoid thinking your needs are the highest priority, and plan accordingly.* Family and work usually trump board responsibilities. Set realistic time lines for action, and remember to follow up regularly. Do whatever you can to simplify the tasks for your overcommitted volunteer.

7. *Share a detailed action plan, broken into baby steps.* Many of us aren't very good at project management. While the steps might seem obvious to you, most board members

don't know what to do first when it comes to fundraising. Hold their hand at every step.

8. *Treat each person individually, with customized expectations.* There are many ways board members can support fundraising, shy of solicitation. Customize activities for that unique person you've come to know (see number 1).

9. *Create a plan for the development of each board member.* Maybe that reluctant board member hasn't had a transforming engagement with your mission. As you would for a donor, craft a strategy for each board member that moves them deeper and deeper into a love affair with your organization. What experiences will move someone up the ladder of giving or participation in fundraising?

10. *Follow up, follow up, follow up.* (See number 5 and number 7.)

11. *Honor board roles and protocols.* Be strategic. Would assistance from board leadership move a reluctant member forward? A peer coach? Regardless of their level of participation, every board member is due the respect of the position. Bad-mouthing one board member to another

is a sure way to undercut the goodwill you'll need to work together.

And finally,

12. *Ask first if board members will use their connections for your organization before you sign them up.* A big mistake many nonprofits make is assuming that if you put someone on the board, they will use their personal or professional connections for your organization. State your desires during the recruitment process. Get the new recruit's consent for your expectations of their service. Failure to ask just leads to disappointment.

Chapter 3: Keep 'Em: Retaining Your Donors with a System for Stewardship

By Pamela Grow

Introduction

Why does your organization need a system for stewardship? Let's take a look at the statistics. According to donor retention expert Penelope Burk, "90% of donors who start contributing to a particular cause stop giving by the fifth renewal request."

And fundraising expert Adrian Sargeant has noted that "eight of ten first-time donors do NOT make a second gift."

You read that right.

Eight of ten first-time donors do NOT make a second gift.

More recent statistics, issued by the Association of Fundraising Processionals and the Urban Institute in their

About Pamela

Are you an accidental fundraiser? Most of us are.

I always trace my start in the nonprofit world to my first job working for a wonderful private family foundation.

I had married, moved to Philadelphia, had two children, and was looking for a part-time job that would still allow me to be at home with my daughters for a few days of the week. The foundation had been established during the 1950s but had only recently begun to establish formal grant policies and procedures. My experiences with that grant-making foundation were wonderful in many respects and exposed me to all the marvelous work being done by nonprofit organizations all over the city, leading me eventually to the world of nonprofit fundraising.

But the truth is I always wanted to make a difference.

As a teenager, I volunteered for progressive political campaigns. Later on, I worked for the Michigan State Legislature—both in the House and the Senate—on issues ranging from social services to mental health to corrections.

We're all doing what we do because we want to make a difference.

Yet there really isn't anything that quite prepares you for working in nonprofit development.

My first job after spending nearly seven years in the relatively cushy foundation world was as a fifteen-hour-per-week—and, yes, $15 an hour—development director for a community agency with a $3M budget.

After a week or so foraging through existing files and talking to everyone and anyone who would sit down with me, I came to the conclusion that nothing had been done for the past five years (since a very successful capital campaign had ended).

No follow-up grant proposals to those generous funders of the capital campaign had been written.

The annual membership campaign had been farmed out to three separate direct mail companies—with disastrous results. Donors were angry. Records were missing. Key community contacts had lapsed.

What a mess!

2011 Fundraising Effectiveness Survey Report, indicate an overall donor retention rate of only 41% in 2010.

And in the 2011 report (*Growing Philanthropy in the United States*) issued by Blackbaud and the Hartsook Institutes for Fundraising, the authors recommend that nonprofits place an enhanced "focus on retention and building supporter loyalty." They note that a "10% improvement in attrition can yield up to a **200% increase in projected value**, as significantly more donors upgrade their giving in multiple ways."

Put simply: Your organization's thank-you letter following your donor's first gift sets the stage for future gifts. Learning how to say "thank you" well—**and often**—is the most effective fundraising tool you have for building sustainable individual funding!

Direct mail guru Mal Warwick has run his Phantom Donor tests in the past, sending out $15, $20, or $25 gifts once or twice a year to a few of the country's top nonprofit organizations to study what comes back in return. When he was thanked, the typical response time was five to seven weeks. Recent "mystery shopping" tests conducted by marketers haven't shown much improvement. Usually, the lack of promptness along with the lack of a thank-you of any kind is cited.

Yet, in today's economy, is merely sending a thank-you letter—and sending it promptly—all it takes?

Stop to think about it for a minute. Why would you waste a prime opportunity to engage your donor on a letter that reads like this thank-you letter to Granny written in typical nonprofit jargon?

Dear Granny,

On behalf of my family and I, I wish to thank you for your generous gift of a pair of socks.

We rely on the generosity derived from birthday presents, Christmas presents, and other gifts from friends and relations which account for 85% of my clothing needs.

I am the only grandchild working towards getting a place at university which is the single greatest means of guaranteeing a future career.

Your thoughtfulness is very encouraging in my work in securing that prized university place

Yours sincerely,

Jack.

This actual thank-you letter from a nonprofit organization (tweaked by Damian O'Brion of Ask Direct), to read as a letter from a grandchild to his grandmother for the gift of a pair of socks, shows just how ridiculous our traditional nonprofit jargon can sound. Lose your formality and write to a friend.

It's funny—but really not so funny when you realize that this is how you and the majority of your peers have been thanking your organization's friends, is it? Because that's what someone who has made the decision to give $10, $20, $250 to your organization is **(a friend)**, and the sooner you learn to treat them as friends, the closer your organization will be to creating lifetime donors.

Why lifetime donors?

Lifetime donors will, in time, become major donors. Today's $1,000 gift given by the CEO's friend (who disappears once the CEO is gone) has nothing on that loyal donor who has given $50 a month every month for the past ten years. Lifetime donors become monthly donors. Lifetime donors leave bequests. Lifetime donors tell their friends and family about the work your organization is doing.

Not convinced yet?

In his timely little book *The Zen of Fundraising*, UK fundraiser Ken Burnett tells the story of a postgraduate student who undertook some research into major donors' attitudes to bequest giving. The student identified meaningful longtime donors who had already made the decision to leave a legacy gift and sent them questionnaires.

One question that was asked of donors was whether they had notified the nonprofit of their choice that a bequest gift was coming. The answers were nearly universal: No. The reason? As one donor wrote: "May change mind."

Let's get busy building lifetime donors!

Getting Started

It's time for a confession of my own.

I'd already been a terrific fundraiser with a fair number of wildly successful appeals under my belt for a number of years before I became enlightened regarding the importance of "knock your socks off" stewardship.

Oh, sure I got my thank-you letters out (and you'd better believe they were prompt). But the majority of my letters, I'm embarrassed to say, read much like our Granny thank-you example.

Yes, typical nonprofit jargon.

The kind of letter the reader glances at, reads midway into the first paragraph, and tosses into their tax receipt file before finishing. Not the kind of response that you want, is it?

Then I had the good fortune to attend a one-day Penelope Burk seminar.

If you're not familiar with Burk's work on donor attrition, you should be. Her book *Donor Centered Fundraising* is considered the landmark classic on how to hold on to your donors.

My thank-you letters became better after reading Burk's book.

Still, it wasn't until I ran across the work of copywriter extraordinaire Lisa Sargent that I became downright insatiable about crafting the perfect thank-you letter. Lisa's *Thank-You Letter Clinic*[1], hosted by SOFII, the showcase of fundraising inspiration, is a wake-up call to all

---

[1] http://www.sofii.org/node/258

nonprofits. In it Lisa dissects the good and the bad of nonprofit thank-you letters and shows you how to make yours better. Her prose sings with gratitude. Imagine the joy your own donors would feel receiving a thank-you letter like Lisa's.

The Ten Essentials of a Perfect Thank- You Letter

1. **Joy.**

   You want, first and foremost, to make the reader—the donor, your friend, your supporter—experience a genuine sense of joy when they open your letter. Envision a tired working mother arriving home early from the office after stopping by the sitter's to pick up her sick three-year-old. She's just listened to fifty minutes of the news on her commute home, all the while worrying about her daughter's fever and frustrated over the time it's taking her to reach her. Daughter falls asleep in the car on the way home, and after tucking her baby into bed, Mom settles in with her mail, off her feet for the first time in hours. Bills, circulars, and your thank-you letter complete her pile. Your donor opens your envelope and reads.

   ○ You are creating miracles!

- Every day, thanks to your support of blah, blah, blah organization. A lonely, homebound senior will receive the gift of food and friendship blah, blah.

Suddenly, your donor is a hero. She's making your work possible, and you've let her know—in no uncertain terms. Somehow her life seems a little less exhausting than it had fifteen minutes ago.

2. **Speed.**

   Speed is of the essence. You must get your thank-you letters out within the first forty-eight hours. No *if*s, *and*s, or *but*s about this. Make it happen! When your dog has an accident on your living room rug, rubbing his nose in it two hours later isn't terribly effective, is it? What system can you put into place to ensure promptness? Thirty minutes a day every day first thing in the morning thanking donors? What will work for your organization?

3. **Personalize it.**

   I'll never forget the day that a consultant from a national firm poo-pooed my insistence on stewardship. "In my opinion, donors are lucky to get a postcard," she said. Don't be that kind of organization. Your thank-you letter (or any correspondence coming from your organization for that matter, including e-mails) should be personalized. These days there is absolutely no excuse for the "dear friend" letter. No excuse.

4. **Reference the amount.**

You should reference the amount in the body of the letter. It's nice to include the date of the gift as well for tax receipt purposes.

5. **Cite the motivation.**

Reference what the gift was toward. Was it an in memoriam gift? An annual appeal gift? A matching gift appeal? And by the way, what are you doing with the donor's money?

6. **Acknowledge past giving.**

Is the donor's past giving acknowledged? If a donor has given every year for the past seven years, you'll want to be sure to let them know how much their continued support means to you.

7. **Include tax-deductible language.**

   Tax-deductible language can be printed in an italic, eight- to ten-point font; centered; below the signature and *PS*.

8. **Don't forget your PS.**

   The PS can be used to drive donors to something new—a Facebook page or a new Twitter account. Perhaps a new blog on your site or your new e-news.

9. **Provide contact info.**

   "If you have any questions or you'd like to stop by and tour our facilities, please call Mary Ann Development at 555-555-0055."

10. **Never, ever, ever ask for a second gift.**

    Now I may change my mind on this one someday. But I highly doubt it. There are two schools of thought on whether an organization should have what's known as a "soft ask" in a donor thank-you letter. You can read the debate between two well-respected fundraisers.[2] According to nearly every recent poll, women are increasingly taking the lead in philanthropic decisions.

---

[2] http://www.sofii.org/node/270

Put simply, women write the checks and are more finely attuned to good etiquette. It simply isn't good manners to include any ask within a thank-you letter—and that includes including a business reply envelope. The sole purpose of your thank-you letter should be to thank your donor. Period.

However, there's no reason why you can't follow up your thank-you letter six weeks later with another thank-you letter—containing information about your monthly giving program.

If you struggle with writing your agency's thank-you letter, relax. Below you'll find a guide to writing the perfect thank-you letter, courtesy of *100 Donors in 90 Days*:[3]

Lisa Sargent's Thank-You Letter Template: Your Step-by-Step Guide to Writing Better Donor Acknowledgments

It confirms you haven't received any goods or services in return for your kind contribution, so please save this letter for tax purposes. You'll also continue to receive our NAME OF newsletter for another year, along with exclusive invitation to educational events. Thanks again, so very much.

---

[3] www.donorluv.com

<Your Masthead>
<Name>
<Address Block>

             <Date>

Dear <Name>,

[Lead Paragraph] Here you'll write a one- to two-line paragraph that draws the donor in, other than "On behalf of . . ." or "Thank you for . . ."

[Paragraph 2] If you haven't thanked above, you can here: "Thank you for your support."

[Paragraph 3] Here you'll write a few lines letting the donor know the gift was received. Include the amount of the donor's gift, date received by your organization, and that it's being put to good use.

[Paragraph 4] In this paragraph, let the donor know about all the great things s/he now makes possible—that is, how, specifically, you're using the gift. An easy way to begin is by saying something like, "Already, your gift is working wonders, providing everything from —— to —— and so much more. Thank you!"

[Paragraph 5] Close with another brief heartfelt thanks. Let the donor know how wonderful s/he is, how you couldn't do what you do without their generosity and kindness. One or two lines.

[Warm Closing] Such as "With my deepest gratitude," as opposed to "Sincerely,"

<President or CEO's name>
<Title, Your Organization Name>

PS [Option 1 – Here you can let the donor know when you'll update them on all they support and how they can reach you. Example: "In the months ahead, you'll receive our XYZ newsletter to update you on all the good work you support. Meanwhile, if you have questions, please call us at XXX-XXX-XXXX or e-mail xyz@your.org." And be sure to thank them more than on time!]

PS [Option 2 – If you must include tax language, try putting it here, but position as a benefit. In this case, you'll move the contact/update paragraph in sample PS above to the main body of the letter. Example: "PS: To conserve resources, this letter serves as your official receipt."]

A Word about Online Gifts

Have you ever walked through your own organization's online giving? Try it. I guarantee you it will be an eye-opening experience.

Think about every step in the donation process. Here's your opportunity to shine!

Where do donors land once they've made a gift? Even if your budget has limited you to using PayPal to accept donations, you can still implement something as simple as a redirect landing page. This is a special page you send donors to after they make a gift. Think about going creative:

- Could your program staff record a one- to two-minute thank-you video?
- What about recording a whiteboard animation thank-you?
- If your agency works with children, what about having your kids create some thank you cards to display?

(Hint: If you're using WordPress, setting up this type of redirect should take you ten minutes tops.)

How can you emulate this wonderful redirect landing page from Best Friends Animal Sanctuary following a gift?

- Thank you so much for your donation of $25.00 to help the animals!

- Your gift brings new life and new hope to a once-sad little face. And you're also helping to spread the message of Best Friends—that kindness to animals builds a better world for all of us. (Option to print receipt on landing page.)

It is short, sweet, and gives a wonderful visual ("once-sad little face").

The follow-up e-mail reads:

- Dear Pamela Grow,

- Thank you so much for your generous gift and for supporting the mission of Best Friends Animal Society.

- There are no fewer than 1,700 animals from all over the country at the sanctuary on any given day; most of them are in need of special attention. Your gift of

$25.00 helps make sure we can give them the best care possible.

- Of course, the work of Best Friends reaches far beyond the sanctuary itself. Best Friends works with communities across the nation to set up No More Homeless Pets programs that will soon bring an end to the killing of abandoned animals in shelters. Check with your local animal shelter to see how you can help further the mission of Best Friends in your own community.

- Kindness to animals makes a better world for all of us. So thank you once again for caring, and may all good things be yours in return for your kindness.

- As a thank-you for your generosity, you will receive an annual subscription to Best Friends magazine to keep you informed on the good news about animals.

- Thank you for making it all possible.

Now there's an example of a terrific thank-you e-mail!

And why not use the opportunity your thank-you e-mail presents to include a message to "like/follow/subscribe to stay current on progress" or even a thank-you video or slideshow?

Donors acquired online tend to have an even lower retention rate than those acquired through direct mail. One way to combat this is by following up your thank-you e-mail with a snail mail thank-you.

Remember, while your online giving may constitute a small portion of your overall giving, that won't always be the case. By putting systems in place now, you'll ensure that your organization's growth in online giving is seamless.

Wow Your Donors

Online retailer Zappos's number 1 family core value is: "Deliver WOW through Service." And do they ever! If you've ever ordered from Zappos, no doubt you've been astounded at their free shipping, their low prices, their exemplary customer service and attention to detail.

Is delivering WOW donor service a number 1 priority with your organization? It should be.

Aside from exemplary stewardship, what are other simple ways that you can WOW your donors?

One very simple habit that you can implement into your day today is something I picked up years ago via change agent Hildy Gottlieb. Hildy penned a marvelous little article called "The Sound a 'Thank You' Makes."[4] Reading that article made a profound difference in how I approached fundraising, and I've made it a point in every fundraising job I've had since reading Hildy's article to schedule thirty minutes into every day to simply pick up the phone and call a few donors.

Regularly survey your donors. Find out what is it about your organization that they like? What would they like to see more of? Surveying donors does not have to be a complex process. Include a question in every e-newsletter. Spend a morning developing a short survey to send out to ten to twenty donors. Post a question on your Facebook page.

Send them gifts. I can hear you now. "What? Are you crazy? We don't have the funds to send donors gifts!" I'm

---

[4] http://www.help4nonprofits.com

not talking about anything expensive. I'm talking about going out on a limb doing something fun and WOW-inducing and bold. When a subscriber to my newsletter recently told me that she was spending the day delivering home-baked goodies to some of her donors, I knew she'd learned her lesson well.

Create a pass-it-on packet. Do you have a limited mailing list? Ask advice of the donors that you do have. Send them packets of information on your agency's work, and ask them to pass them along to friends, family, or neighbors who might share their interest.

Get your board involved, either in calling donors or in writing personal thank-you notes. Several of my clients regularly distribute note cards—along with the names, suggested scripts, and gift amounts of one or two donors. Some schedule small thanking parties during board meetings.

Welcome kits play an excellent role in educating your new donors to your organization. Typically, your welcome package would go beyond a mere thank-you letter to include items such as photographs, surveys, a benefits brochure, even a small gift such as a bookmark. Send them in an oversized envelope marked with a bold *Welcome!*

Gratitude Reports. Instead of the usual annual report, think about creating a *gratitude report*[5] like the one Agents of Good developed for their client.

Can your clients thank your donors in special ways? Check out the very special (and much appreciated) way that Sunday Friends is thanking donors.[6]

What additional opportunities do you have to WOW your donors? Get creative! Think of different holidays when you could send out a simple card. I like to shower donors with love on Valentine's Day. Sending out a thank-you card the week of Thanksgiving creates more of an impact than a Christmas/Hanukkah card because it's unexpected (but oh so appropriate). And don't forget birthdays.

I worked for the State of Michigan's House of Representatives for a number of years. One state representative, who shall remain nameless, was such a holy terror that she had long ago given up on hiring an

---

[5] http://blog.agentsofgood.org/2010/02/24/featured-project-interval-house-gratitude-report/
[6] http://www.youtube.com/watch?v=2MmZxB_I20A

actual staff member and used a temp agency instead. She was heartily disliked by staff and colleagues alike but beloved by her constituents (she never was voted out of office and served until her retirement). Why? She made it a point to obtain her constituents' birth dates and send out birthday cards to each and every one of them.

Don't have the technology or resources to implement this? Facebook to the rescue! Use the Facebook friends' birthday reminder, and spend all of five minutes every morning wishing your organization's friends a happy birthday.

Using Social Media for Stewardship
Yes, you can! Stewarding your donors should play a regular role in your organization's social media.

Ask yourself, "What would happen if I thanked one donor every day for the next year?" Create quick YouTube thank-yous! (I recommend that every nonprofit organization owns a Flip-cam.) You can also thank your donors publicly on both Twitter and Facebook (just be sure they haven't asked to remain anonymous).

Creating Your Stewardship System

By creating actual systems for thanking your donors, you've taken a proactive step toward nurturing and retaining your organization's donors—a step that will pay off big-time in the long run!

Whether you're a new organization and you've yet to receive an in-memoriam gift, or a foundation grant, or even an online donation, you'll want to begin now creating letters for every eventuality. Using a binder for your organization's thank-you letters is my favorite method of staying organized. Review your thank-you letters on a quarterly (or, at bare minimum, twice yearly) basis, and update them with your latest accomplishments.

Commit to thanking one donor every day, and create a calendar of opportunities for WOWing your donors throughout the year. Remember, your job is to utterly delight donors!

A Checklist for Stewardship

☐ Is your thank-you letter mailed within forty-eight hours of receipt of gift? What procedures can you put into place to make it so?

☐ Are you calling donors on a regular basis?

- ☐ Are you showering your donors with joy?

- ☐ Did you reference the gift amount in the body of the letter?

- ☐ Did you use the word *you* more often than not?

- ☐ If they're a new donor, did you welcome them to your organization's family?

- ☐ Is your letter personalized?

- ☐ Did you let the donor know when they should expect to hear from you?

- ☐ Did you say thank you more than once?

- ☐ Is your thank-you letter hand-signed?

- ☐ Did you include the contact information for a key staff person?

- ☐ Did you include a PS?

- ☐ Are you making it a practice to regularly map out the donor's experience when they make a gift to your organization?

Skip this chapter at your organization's peril. Take it to heart and watch how cultivating an attitude of gratitude works like a domino effect in growing your organization's donor database.

Chapter 4: Sharing Stories
By Lori L. Jacobwith

Storytelling is an ancient practice of conveying events in words, images, and sounds. Stories have been shared in every culture as a means of entertainment, education, preservation of culture, and to instill knowledge, values, and morals.

As human beings, we have been communicating with one another through storytelling since we lived in caves and sat around campfires.

The truth is we are connected to others through the stories we tell or they share with us. You may not always remember the facts about how many homeless there are in your city, but you ARE likely to remember the feeling you had about the story of the family who is homeless and the day-to-day struggles in their life.

One of the most powerful ways to connect people to your mission is to paint a picture with your words, which allows the listener or reader to feel something about the work of your organization. The easiest way to do this is by sharing an example of how your work affects one man, woman, or

About Lori

When I was young, I was known as the helper. I babysat and watched over the kids in my neighborhood. I worked to make my mom's life easier raising four kids. Eventually, I realized I wanted to be governor of Minnesota so I could help lots of people.

After graduating from college, I spent time working on two political campaigns: a U.S. Senate campaign and a gubernatorial campaign. I was thrilled to be working for the governor and to see firsthand what the job truly was.

I quickly found that being governor meant spending lots of time doing "donor/voter" stewardship and raising money. Both of the politicians I worked with were amazing communicators who taught me the value of sharing stories about real people.

I soon realized I wanted to be able to see the impact of my fundraising up close and personal. After learning about fundraising from the fire hose of political campaigns, I eventually took my fundraising skills to the social profit sector.

As a development director and executive director for organizations doing amazing work, I was truly able to watch the funds I raised help real people every day.

After three development jobs for small organizations and one large university department, I raised millions that moved the organizations from being overdependent on grant proposals to having successful annual fund campaigns. Each time, I was able to grow the annual fund exponentially during my time there.

I believe it was the magic of sharing stories with our donors that deepened their commitment and increased their giving.

Before I launched my own training and coaching business in 2006, I spent five years traveling the country as a senior manager for a large fundraising training company. I got to train thousands of staffs and board members. Since 2001, my work has helped organizations raise more than $200 million from individual donors.

My mission is to help organizations raise more money from individuals. My vision is to help you do that with ease.

child. Sharing that example and painting a picture of the life of one person is a story.

> **In the presence of a true story, we say, "Yes, this is how it feels; this is how it would happen; this is what one might think."**
> **—Daniel Taylor,**
> ***The Power of Personal Storytelling***

I've listened to and retold thousands of stories throughout my career. I've found that the secret to retelling a story is to make the effort to fill in the words that are NOT BEING SPOKEN. Insert words that will cause others to feel something.

This chapter provides coaching to help you find and share stories. After reading it, my intention is that you'll find it easier to hunt for and share a story that is emotionally connecting, causes the listener to feel something, and in turn causes the listener to want to take action on behalf of the person you are talking about.

It's simple really. People give their time, money, and advice to organizations they feel emotionally connected to. So telling a story about how you change the lives of real people is critical for generating more funds for your organization.

Often board members and some staff become removed from the work of the organization or become "hardened" to emotionally wrenching stories.

This is not to say you should cry and feel awful each time you tell a story. Whether you are an advocacy, education, environmental, human service, arts, or any other type of nonprofit organization, you affect the lives of real people.

As you go through the worksheets and suggestions in the next few pages, make sure you are connecting to WHY that person or story means something to you.

It is important to build your muscles in this area. And that means practicing sharing stories both verbally and in written form. You'll want to share your stories often, in different settings, and invite feedback so you can truly move them from boring to brilliant.

Let's get started.

Mission Moments

I define a *mission moment* as any example of how your organization is making an impact. It's an example about a real person, family, or human situation. It can be:

- a board member telling how it felt to participate at your recent fundraising event;
- a staff person talking about the family that got turned away that day;
- a volunteer saying *thank you* for allowing them to "work" with your organization;
- a client saying *thank you* for helping them to make a life change;
- an elected official sharing what a difference your legislation will make; or
- a student giving you that smile of gratitude after you've helped her fill out financial aid papers.

Mission moments are often short inspirational examples of your work.

Mission moments put a face on what you do. They are stories and examples that can be repeated by others because they are not too long. They are inspiring and often give visibility to something you'd like to do more of but, due to limited resources, you simply can't.

Where to find good stories to share?

Asking people to share a story often means getting a deer-in-the-headlights look of fear.

And then the words start to tumble out: "Um, but, I don't meet any of our clients."
"I don't know any stories about our work."
"Gee, the program staff are the ones who know our clients, but when I ask them to tell me stories, they give me one line, or they ignore me."

If this sounds like YOU, read on.

The magic in finding stories is twofold.

1.   What you ask.

2.   Who you ask.

What you ask:

If your program staff truly DOES have the only access to your clients and you want stories about the impact of your work, here are some questions to ask:

- Who did you turn away last week? Tell me about one of those people or families.

- What person, family, child, senior, or fill-in-the-blank has stayed on your mind this week? What circumstance led them to ask for our services? What are we doing to help them? What are we not able to do for them?

- What is your favorite thing about this person? Why do you want to help them?

- Have you met anyone lately who made you incredibly proud that we exist? Tell me about them and how YOU have inadvertently or directly helped them.

Rather than asking staff (especially program staff) for stories, ask them these or other open-ended questions. A great way to begin building your pool of stories is to start a staff meeting with one of these questions. At the start of the staff meeting, flesh out one real-life example of how your organization is making a difference saving or changing lives.

Help your team help you collect and share real-life examples of the people's lives you are saving and changing.

The truth is you'll have to ask a few questions to fully flesh out the important parts of the story. But using the template and story-building criteria provided here, you will soon find it easier to identify a powerful mission moment that you can turn into an emotionally connecting example to share with others.

Who you ask:

Asking your colleagues (especially the frontline staff) the questions listed here WILL help you capture more and better quality information for your story sharing.

When I've worked at organizations where we provided a direct service, I would make sure to put myself in a position at least once a month to be around those we served. I sat in the lobby area at the Department of Ophthalmology and visited with patients; I took the phone calls from parents whose children had just been diagnosed with juvenile diabetes; I attended volunteer trainings. I got out of my office and made sure to connect one-on-one with people to learn their story.

Permission to share the stories is key, but once YOU have established a relationship with someone, that permission is an easier process to navigate through.

I believe you can ask your open-ended questions to LOTS of other people. There are many other people who have great stories about how your organization is doing amazing work.

Here's a list of who to ask to get you started (you'll want to add to this list as other groups of people come to mind):

WHO TO ASK	OPEN-ENDED QUESTIONS TO GET YOU STARTED
People you serve	• What was your life like before you came here? • How has our team helped you? • What is your life like now?
Their family members	• What differences have you seen in your loved one's life since they came to us?
Board members and former members	• Why did you join our board? • What is the most important part of our work for you? • Do you have a special mission moment you remember about someone you met who was helped by our organization?

First-time or longtime donors	• Why did you start or continue to make a financial gift to us? • What is special for you about our work? • Do you have a special mission moment you remember about someone you met who was helped by our organization?*
Other staff	• Do you have a special mission moment you remember about someone you met who was helped by our organization?
Foundations	• Why have you funded our programs? • What is different/special about our work that compels your foundation to make a grant?
Event sponsors	• What do you know about our work? • Why do you make a financial gift to us? • Do you have a special mission moment you remember about someone who was helped by our organization?
Vendors	• What do you know about our work? • Do you have a special mission moment that you remember about someone you met who was helped by our organization?
Elected officials	• What do you know about our work? • Do you have a special mission moment that you remember about someone you met who was helped by our organization?

Lori's Storytelling Criteria

In order to put together the framework to share powerful stories, you'll want to use these four criteria to build the foundation of your story:

1. **Tell a story about an actual person using name, age, and other descriptors to help your listener visualize.** Here is where painting a picture with your words is key. A story about a seven-year-old is heard differently than a story of a twenty-seven-year-old. Share ages and physical characteristics so others can see this person as you talk about them.

2. **Use words that emotionally connect the listener to your work and the person you're speaking about. No jargon.** You may find that you don't even notice the jargon. So share your story with someone outside your organization, preferably someone young, even a teenager. Ask them to tell you what parts of the story they liked and which parts didn't make sense. You'll be surprised how well you can limit or eliminate the agency jargon with others' help.

3. **Share specific examples of YOUR work** and how it makes a difference in the life of a real person. This

is the part of storytelling that is often skipped or where we are skimpy with our description. Your staff or that volunteer made something happen by listening and caring, or planting something, or connecting someone. Don't skimp here!

4. **When telling a story, it must be short—two minutes or less.** If you are creating a story for a newsletter, or annual report, or even for your website, you have more leeway with the time and number of words. However, when you are *telling* a story, the key is to keep it very short and powerful. Leave the listener wanting more and asking you questions. THAT'S how you deepen engagement.

Now that you are clear on the key elements, let's walk through how you build the story. Take your time working through this process. Invite your team to do these steps with you.

Create your brilliant, emotionally connecting story.

1. **Identify one person** (only one) who stands out for you as someone who has benefitted from your programs, has been a real success story for your organization, OR could have been a success if you had more resources.

2. **Learn and list their first name, age, and describe some characteristics of their personality or appearance.**

3. **Write down all of the exact results** that man, woman, or child got from being served by your organization. Be very specific. Did he get a job? Stop drinking or using drugs? Did she get her diploma? Did that child have someone to trust for the very first time? Did that teenager start to make choices that were not harmful?

4. **Next, make a list of the *transformations* that flowed from those results.** Take some time and make the list as long as possible. Make sure to use words that are feeling words rather than "reporting" words. For some ideas on *feeling* words, see the list included later in this chapter.

Did the teenager who finally had someone who trusted them get better grades in school? Spend less time suspended? Feel like she fit in better? Begin to look and feel differently because her self-confidence and energy were higher?

5. **You now have a list that includes many words and phrases that are perfect for crafting your story.** Underline the words that resonate with you—that cause you to feel something.

Now you can put those words and phrases together to begin to tell the three parts of the story:

a) What was life like before your organization became involved?

b) What happened when your organization got involved?

c) What is life like now? (Show the hope and future here OR show how the ending that is not finished could be changed with more time, support, and resources given to your organization.)

Here's a short example from my own work as a development director at the Department of Ophthalmology at the University of Arizona:

Sample Story

A woman with keratoconus was helped by our organization. Over the years, no doctors had been able to help her with her vision problems. Finally, an ophthalmologist in her community who had been trained by our doctors recently performed cornea transplant surgery on her. She's always wanted to have better vision, and after her doctor performed surgery, she can see better.

Lori's Version of the Story

Sondra is twenty-seven and lives in Sonora, Mexico, just south of Tucson where the Department of Ophthalmology is located. She's a tall woman with long brown hair. But there is no spring in her step or smile on her face. She's been in need of cornea transplant surgery all her life. I'm not exactly sure what that surgery is, but I know that when Sondra wakes up each morning and looks in the mirror as she's washing her face, the mirror is cloudy, as if there is soap on it. And there is no color. The very blurry images she sees are black and white.

With contributions from our supporters, we have created an international fellows program where we teach doctors from other countries how to perform cornea transplant surgery. Dr. Rodriguez, Sondra's doctor, was the first recipient of our fellows program. When he was fully trained, he decided to offer one surgery to his community for free each year. Sondra was his first recipient.

She was very grateful to us for training her doctor because on the day of her surgery, *she was able to see the faces of her seven- and nine-year-old sons for the very first time.*

Now Sondra works outside her home and feels a freedom she's never felt before. Her smile lights up a room, and there is a sparkle in her eye of gratitude and love for the Department of Ophthalmology and her favorite doctor.

One of my favorite resources for help in creating a powerful story comes from Katya Andresen's blog:[7]

The Four Parts of a Great Story

by Mark Rovner

1. **A relatable protagonist.** That means an individual (the main character), not a group or institution! The protagonist has to be facing something with which we can relate. What unites us all are the trials and tribulations of being human.

---

[7] http://nonprofitmarketingblog.com/

2. **Lots of conflict.** Conflict is story oxygen. The more conflict, the more engaging the story.

3. **A loathsome villain.** Name names, or make clear what tough obstacle is in the way of our hero.

4. **Telling details.** If a story element can't connect with one of the five senses, be suspicious of it.

Words and Phrases That Evoke Emotion

There are many, many words that will do a good job of evoking emotion. This list was created to help get you started crafting your story and to spark more words. Notice words throughout your day that cause you to feel something, and incorporate those into the stories you share.

Remember, though, the placement of these words and phrases is key to creating a powerful story.

A place to call my own	Blessed
Abandoned	Bright
Ashamed	Catapult
Awkward	Delight

Emotionally bruised

Empower

Erupt in anger

Even out the odds

Explosive anger

Exuberant

Eyes pooled with tears

Fleeting feelings of _____

Gentle

Glowing smile

Gnarly hands

Healthy

Joy

Kind

Leathery hands/skin

Lifeline

Overcome

Passionate

Precious

Ravenous

Revitalize

Safe

Surrender

Thrive

Tired eyes

Uncomfortably shy

Vibrant

Weary

Weathered face

Putting it all together, here is a simple template to begin drafting your story:

Let me tell you about _____

_____.

(Fill in name, age, and some descriptive details.)

His/her life was _____

_____.

(Share specific details about how they felt about their choices, unasked-for situation, health issue, etc. You get the idea.) Special note: Stay away from jargon.

[Name] made her way to us because _____

_____.

(Share how the person found you or your programs and what happened once they arrived. Be specific. Maybe ten other homeless shelters turned them down, or their doctor or landlord referred them to you.)

And now _____'s [name] is _____

_____

_____.

(Make sure the listener has that aha moment of why your work is important. Insert emotionally connecting words and real examples of how life is different.)

What if your organization provides work in the area of advocacy or the environment, or you are an umbrella organization that provides no direct service? You may be thinking, "We don't have a mission moment to fit into this storytelling template."

I say you do.

If one person's life has been touched by your work, then tell that story. You have to seek out the people who can share with you why your work has mattered to them, but ultimately, you DO have a story, or ten, or one hundred to share.

You got involved with your organization because you saw something special. The examples you share with others should cause that same sort of feeling.

Maya Angelou said it best: "People will forget what you said. People will forget what you did. But people will never forget how you made them feel."

Additional Resources:

For more support in crafting powerful stories, download Lori's free e-book at www.boring2brilliant.com.

- "Imagine What's Possible: Step-by-Step Storytelling System": http://www.lorijacobwith.com/storytellingsystem

- Free Resources: http://www.lorijacobwith.com/free-resources

- Ignited Online Fundraising Community: http://www.lorijacobwith.com/membership

- Other Resources: http://www.lorijacobwith.com/store

Chapter 5: Growing Awareness
By Kirsten Bullock, CFRE, MBA

It's more important than ever to raise awareness and introduce more people to your cause. The primary reason: If people don't know about the needs of the community and your organization, they won't become involved (or donate). In this chapter, you'll learn the three aspects of a communications plan, including your audience (market), your story (message), and how you'll communicate with people (media). In addition, you'll learn about how to pull that into an overall plan.

As strategy goes, I've found that the traditional marketing funnel is the easiest way to explain how the pieces fit together as it aims to move people from Awareness through Consideration and Preference to Action and Loyalty. Nonprofit communication also aims for action and

About Kirsten

I was exposed to nonprofits from a very young age, as most of my summers were spent at a camp for kids with physical disabilities. My mom was the camp nurse and my dad the camp director. That, combined with a brother who had muscular dystrophy, has been a driving force for me as I strive to invest back in the world.

It was at an arts school in North Carolina, majoring in Stage Management, when I was first introduced to philanthropy. Four years later, when I was working toward my bachelor's degree in Social Work, I ended up completing my internship at the foundation at a local hospital, and I was hooked.

After taking a break to complete my MBA, I returned to nonprofits as the development director for a community health center. It was there that I experienced the thrill of growing a development program from the ground up. In a three-year-time period, we went from $200,000 to just over $1.3 million in charitable funds raised.

Since that time, I've had the honor and privilege to speak to and work with hundreds of organizations. These have ranged from small local start-ups to multimillion dollar organizations.

Now, through my work with *The NonProfit Academy™*, I'm able to have a positive impact on thousands of organizations and, I believe, make the world a better place.

loyalty. If people are aware that there is a need, they can consider various ways to address that need (whether through existing organizations or on their own). They select their preference and then take action (volunteering, donating, or engaging in some other work). Ideally, they will become advocates for the organization and increase their involvement (perhaps by encouraging others to become involved with the organization or through a planned gift).

As you start to think about raising awareness for your organization, keep in mind that each of your activities should fit somewhere in this funnel. Everything in your communications plan should be helping to create stronger relationships that result in gifts or other contributions to the organization.

In addition, always have a call to action. And by a call to action I mean one call to action, any more can confuse readers. Deep down, I believe everyone wants to help! So make it clear in your message what you need, make it easy to respond, and be sure to say thank you. Often.

Communications and marketing doesn't need to be expensive. Creativity can go a long way in gaining attention from the media. Katya Andresen shares in her blog[8] about a nonprofit in Seattle that adopted a chicken (trying to cross the road) as a way to build awareness. The vision of

---

[8] http://www.nonprofitmarketingblog.com/comments/help_i_have_n o_marketing_budget/

Feet First was to make their community more walkable. They built a whole campaign around "helping the chicken cross the road" and raised visibility for it by sending someone out—dressed as a chicken—to attempt to cross the road in various spots around the city. They raised visibility for their cause—and raised the money they needed.

We live in a generous society, and people want to support those causes with which they are engaged and passionate. By raising awareness and inviting people to engage in the organization, you will be one step closer to having the money to fulfill your mission.

Planning

There are several possibilities available as you begin to communicate about your organization. It can be easy to fall into a scattershot approach. Pretty soon, you are doing about thirty different things (and none of them very well). Having a written plan can help you get focused—and help you start getting the results you're really looking for.

There are four components you'll want to identify as part of your overall communications plan. First, identify your goal. This helps both in planning and in the ability of measuring whether or not you're having the impact you intended. Next is to create your message. Third is to create your plan. Finally, you'll select the strategies to accomplish your goal.

It would be easy to spend a lot of time on any of the vehicles outlined in this chapter, so you'll want to focus on a maximum of three to five to start. This chapter will provide some basics for you to start developing some awareness strategies.

Here are the broad strokes of your plan that can be tracked in a simple table:

- **Target markets** – With whom will you communicate?
- **Goals** – What do you want them to do?
- **Strategies** – How will you encourage them to do that, and what vehicles will you use?
- **Metrics** – How will you know you've accomplished your goal?
- **Person Responsible** – Who will ensure the task is completed?
- **Status** – How are activities progressing? This converts the plan from something that sits on the shelf to something that will be shared at every board meeting (and/or staff meeting) and will be a dynamic, useful document.

Goals

As you select your strategies and begin to develop your plan, keep in mind that there should be an overarching goal that you are trying to accomplish, as well as a goal for each communication piece you send out. When marketing a nonprofit organization, there are generally three primary goals you might have: general awareness, building credibility, and increasing engagement.

First, to increase awareness, **educate the community about the need**. If potential advocates do not recognize there is a challenge, they won't become engaged in it.

Next, to increase the possibility of your organization being selected as the way to address the community need, **build the organization's credibility**. You'll want to make the case that your organization is the best one suited to address the challenge(s) you've claimed.

Third, **help your audience increase their engagement with your organization** by making a gift, volunteering, or becoming involved in some other way. To accomplish that, each piece should include a call to action of some sort.

You'll be increasing awareness, recruiting more advocates of your organization, finding new volunteers, and/or increasing donations. Whatever the goal, include an appropriate call to action, and try to build in a way to measure the success of the campaign.

As part of this process, you'll also be identifying the audience with which you are trying to communicate. The more you know about them, the easier it will be to target your message.

Message

Once you have a goal and your audience established, it becomes easier to develop your message. As is illustrated in this story, it's important to be clear and to ensure that your reader (or listener) understands your message:
If you've been following my writing for a while, you have probably read about my brother Frits. He always had great insights and was able to see the humorous side of things. Frits had muscular dystrophy, was a quadriplegic, and was confined to a wheelchair for much of his life. He passed away in 2003. Here's a short story I loved to hear him tell (in Frits's words):

> A couple years ago (in 2001), I had a nurse with a fairly heavy accent. It was morning, and as is often the case, I needed to wipe my eyes. So I asked Mildred (not her real name), "Will you please wipe

my eyes?" So she went to the closet to get some tissue, but she also came back with a couple of gloves. I thought nothing of it because I figured some people would rather use a glove. But then, she went to start turning me over. Confused, I said again, "I need to wipe my eyes," trying to emphasize my words very clearly so she could understand me better. Again, she started to turn me over. I said, "No, I need to wipe my eyes." Then all of a sudden, she started to laugh. She finally understood me. Amidst her laughing, she said to me that she thought I had said, "I need to wipe my a——." Very funny.

So much can be lost in translation—and pronunciation.

When you describe what your organization does and the issues you address, what type of words are you using? Do you use a lot of acronyms? Buzzwords that only those in your industry understand? Terms like *recidivism*, *myocardial infarction*, *planned giving*, etc.?

As you're developing your message, let someone who is not in your industry read it and give you feedback. Better yet, tell a fifth grader what you do; then write that down and use it instead. It doesn't mean talking down to your readers, it simply makes it easier for them to read.

Vehicles

Once you know your target audience and message, you can start taking a look at the best medium with which to communicate. In this section, we'll cover a few of the vehicles that are available to you. Don't feel as if you need to do everything—you'd just get overwhelmed. I've often heard people talk about the "crawl, walk, run" philosophy. Basically, it acknowledges that we all need to start somewhere.

Nonprofit Marketing Trends

Before we go deeper into the possible strategies you might want to use, here is some information about how other nonprofit organizations are using marketing techniques.

The *Nonprofit Communications Trends Report*[9] includes a survey question related to how organizations ranked each of the following communication tools.

Communication Tool	% of Those Who Ranked the Tool *Very* or *Somewhat* *Important*	
	2011	**2012**
Website	96%	93%
E-mail Marketing/E-mail Newsletters	94%	89%

[9] 2011 and 2012 *Nonprofit Communications Trends Report*, available at http://nonprofitmarketingguide.com/2011trends.

Facebook	79%	80%
In-Person Events	67%	66%
Print (Newsletters-Direct Mail)	67%	67%
Media Relations/Public Relations (PR)	57%	57%
Twitter	34%	34%
Blog	27%	27%
Video (YouTube, etc.)	26%	30%
Paid Advertising	21%	17%
Phone Calls/Phone Banks	17%	19%
Photo Sharing	11%	6%
Audio (e.g., podcasts)	6%	4%
Texting	4%	4%

Frequency of mailing and e-mailing is a topic that comes up fairly often. There are several nonprofit leaders I've talked to who resist sending more than quarterly contacts to their constituents. It doesn't seem that the respondents to this survey had any qualms regarding frequent communications as 72% of respondents to the survey indicated that they e-mailed at least monthly. The 2012 report indicates that this has increased to 78%. In order to stay top of mind with our donors we need to stay in touch on a frequent basis. In my opinion this means at least monthly, whether by e-mail or mail.

I'll be covering some of the main ideas related to each strategy. If you need additional help/support related to these, there are several how-to videos and support networks all over the web. A few good sources I've found include NonprofitMarketingGuide.com, SocialBrite.com, NTEN.org, and AhernComm.com.

Online Vehicles

Social media and other online vehicles are not strategies in and of themselves. They are simply additional communication vehicles available to you.

Website

Main point? Your website is the central point for all of your online activity. The majority of people who make a gift online do so from the organization's website—and if their curiosity is piqued by your social media activities, they will find their way to your website. So start here if you do not have a website already.

Financial cost? An ad-supported website can be free, however it's recommended that you pay for hosting so you can have control over the messages your visitors see. Depending on the size and the complexity of the site, you can pay anywhere from $50 per year to a few hundred dollars per month for hosting. I've seen complex websites that were $80,000–$100,000, but most small nonprofits have no need for that type of complexity. Some notable nonprofit websites include CharityWater.com, StJude.org, WiserGirls.org, and Amnesty.org.

Time cost? Whether you build it yourself or have someone build it for you, content development takes time. Review what other successful websites do and imitate them. If you must build it yourself, WordPress is an easy and free option that is available. You don't need to be technically savvy to make changes and updates to your content. Joomla is another popular website platform.

Who will you reach? Anyone with web access might find your website. However most people will need to be directed to the website somehow. This could be through print messages, e-newsletters, ads, search engines, etc.

What format can the message take? The format is very flexible if you know HTML, WordPress, Joomla or whichever other platform you choose.

Best use? To provide a general overview of the organization and provide opportunities for people to become engaged with the organization. You can create unique landing pages for the campaigns you run. Just remember, your website is a destination, not an awareness strategy in and of itself. In order to keep people coming back to your site, you'll need to continually provide new, interesting content and communicate about that content using other communication vehicles.

E-mail Marketing/Newsletter

Are you wondering if e-mails are getting your message through to your audience? Have you been postponing growing your e-mail correspondence? Convio released results from a 2011 study,[10] which suggests increased e-mail correspondence has a positive impact on giving.

Convio partnered with the ASPCA to test some different strategies. Those donors who received e-mails in addition to other communications gave more than those who did not receive e-mails. Here's what they found:

- Gave 112% more on and offline

---

[10] *The Next Generation of American Giving* available at http://www.convio.com/signup/next-generation/next-generation-resources.html.

- Gave 85% more gifts
- Saw a 54% increase in recency
- 15–20% higher average gift

Main point? Regular e-mail correspondence helps you build credibility and trust with your supporters. As you can see from the results of the study referenced above, it can also positively impact giving.

One of the biggest challenges marketers face is building an opt-in e-mail list. It's not recommended that you purchase e-mail lists. Some better ways to build your list include:

- Adding a signature line to your e-mails that directs the recipient to a sign-up box on your website.
- Collecting e-mail addresses at public events with a simple form handed out to each attendee.
- Including a subscription opt-in on your website. As an incentive, offer a relevant, interesting report to people who subscribe.

Financial cost? Minimal (from zero to about $100+ per month depending on the size of your e-mail list). Using a management system for your e-mail campaigns may cost a little, but the time you save versus trying to manually keep a list updated is well worth it. A management system can help you track click-throughs, manage bounces, track what information people are responding to, and adjust future e-mails accordingly. Some of the most popular ones include Constant Contact, Vertical Response, AWeber, and MailChimp. More donor databases are also integrating this capability into their programs.

Time cost? This will change depending on your annual strategy. But it is possible to keep it really simple. A beginning approach might include a monthly two- to three-paragraph update, while a more developed program could include weekly correspondence with variable content based on interests and a monthly e-newsletter.

Who will you reach? You will reach anyone who shares their e-mail address with you. Let me restate the importance of not purchasing e-mail addresses. First, most of the reputable e-mail management companies will not let you upload a purchased list. Secondly, once your e-mail gets flagged as spam, it's really difficult to get off the list. Lastly, sending unsolicited e-mail will not be positively looked at by your supporters.

What format can the message take? The message can take just about any—from a simple letter to a full-blown designed e-mail.

Your first task is to identify what it is your donors and prospects want. Talk to them, ask them, and then provide the information they are looking for via e-mail on a frequent basis. If you wait too long between e-mails, people tend to forget that they signed up for the list. And guess what they do when that happens? You get marked as spam. Communicate regularly and with good information the reader will find interesting and that won't happen.

While you're at it, take a look at your website too. Are you sharing stories? Do you share about how your donors are changing lives or is it simply an online brochure that lists what you do? Hint: People are generally more intrigued by stories and transformed lives.

Best use? E-mail communication is very flexible. E-mails can simply convey information, or they can also include polls, links to surveys, etc.

E-mail does not replace your need to communicate with your donors in print. You'll see the best results when you include both print and online communications.

Social Media: Facebook/Twitter/LinkedIn/Google+

Main point? Social media is best used connecting with donors you already have and encouraging them to share information about you via their social networks. Social media, especially Twitter, can also be a good way to get a quick pulse of what people are talking about.

Before you jump into using social media, you'll benefit from spending some time listening and watching how others are using the media. Different online groups have different cultures related to self-promotion and you want to make sure you are adhering to the norms of the group. Because the use of this media is still emerging, you'll also want to watch and see what other nonprofits are doing to stay attuned to best practices as they develop.

Financial cost? While there is zero financial cost to get started, there are some paid advertising options on social media platforms including Facebook, LinkedIn and Twitter.

Time cost? If you're not careful, you can spend an extensive amount of time online with absolutely zero return. Be sure you know your goals ahead of time and you'll be able to invest your time wisely.

Twitter: Productive Tool or Waste of Time?

I think the jury's still out on this one. A handful of organizations have had great success with fundraising, but the majority have yet to see tangible results.

But just because something is not directly related to immediate dollars doesn't mean that there isn't a long-term financial impact.

A few years ago, I was serving as the statewide development director for an international organization. In an effort to connect with our donors (some for the very first time), we asked some of our board members to host gatherings in different locations around the state. Our contributors loved it.

In some cases, this was the first direct interaction they had with anyone related to the charity. And there was no money raised.

But over the next six months, gifts by people who had attended these gatherings contributed a total of 70% more than they had given the prior year. A success? I think so. Any tool that helps us build a closer relationship with our donors can have a long-term impact. So instead of asking whether Twitter is a waste of time, maybe we should redefine what we're expecting.

Who will you reach? Through social media you can potentially reach anyone who is *active* on that particular platform, however it will most likely be limited to those people you are already connected to in some way.

What format can the message take? Updates, messages to your members, longer messages, polls, surveys, and other interactive formats. While a tweet is limited to 140 characters there is an ability to attach a photo. Two tools you may want to explore include TwitLonger and TwitPic.

Best use? By creating a community, and by connecting your supporters to one another, you are building an engaged group of potential advocates and potential donors. Facebook in and of itself is not a fundraising strategy, rather an engagement strategy that can lead to donations.

Remember, social media doesn't replace your need to collect e-mail addresses and snail mail addresses. Social media platforms are owned by someone else, which means they can and have changed the rules about how you engage with your followers. This could leave you scrambling if you don't have a backup plan for communicating with your supporters.

Blogging

Main point? Blogs can help build a closer connection with visitors to your website. There is also an SEO benefit to posting new content on your website. Your blog should be integrated into your current site to make it easier for people to find it.

Financial cost? There is no cost as your blog is integrated into your website.

Time cost? While the writing can be time consuming, with practice it gets easier. You can engage other staff members and volunteers to write posts to minimize your time commitment. You will want to take it seriously and publish posts on a frequent basis. Having a blog and not updating it can look like an abandoned store that still has a sign up.

Who will you reach? People who visit your website or follow your blog through an RSS feed. You can also encourage visitors to your blog to share the posts with their social network.

What format can the message take? The format is flexible. You can chose to compile content that others have written or develop your own. Infographics, stories, and pictures can also be created and used as part of your blog.

Best use? Define what it is you're hoping to get from the medium; then work toward that goal. If you're not a writer, recruit someone who is—or one who can help you improve your writing.

Off-Line/Traditional Strategies

Print

Main points? With mail, it can be easy to get lost in the pile. Keep it simple, direct, and make it easy for someone to make a gift or get involved. Costs can add up, so make sure you're sending to the right list.

Financial cost? Direct mail can get expensive, you'll need to keep in mind:

- Content creation
- Design
- Mailing lists
- Printing
- Processing (if you use a mail house)
- Postage—you can save money by mailing at the nonprofit rate, but allow plenty of time for delivery as it goes out at the convenience of the post office. Also, make sure you adhere to post office guidelines regarding weight, size, etc., as irregular pieces can increase the price significantly.

Time cost? Your time investment will include planning the campaign, creating content, printing, and sorting. Some of this time can be saved by using a mail house. Often the costs associated with using a mail house are offset by qualifying for a lower postage rate.

Who will you reach? You can reach anyone for whom you have a mailing address.

What format can the message take? Fairly flexible. If possible, it's a good idea to create an overall campaign and integrate your mailing with an online component. This increases the possibility of a positive response.

Best use? The best use of direct mail is to stay in contact with current supporters and augment online campaigns. With direct mail there is also the potential of reaching a new group of people you are not currently interacting with, however as direct mail response rates have decreased this has become a more costly option. In fact, many direct marketers are now saying that it can take up to five years to break even on a new direct mail campaign.

In-Person Introductory Events

Main points? The main purpose of introductory events is to introduce your organization to new people, most likely friends and colleagues of your current supporters. These are short events, typically one to two hours, where attendees are given some basic information about the organization. This includes a tour where possible and may or may not include an ask for a gift. They can be hosted by the organization or by current supporters.

Financial cost? The cost of these small awareness gatherings is minimal as the hosts of the gatherings often cover incidentals and food. When hosted by the organization, light snacks may be needed. It may make sense to invest in a good video about the organization to help share your story.

Time cost? The time investment to run an introductory event is fairly limited. Preparation for the first one will some time as you will need to develop the presentation and support materials for your host. These materials can be reused as you recruit additional hosts.

Who will you reach? As with social media, you will be connecting with friends and associates of people you are connected with already. This includes board members, volunteers, staff members and even current donors.

What format can the message take? The format for these events can be somewhat flexible. It could be anything from an informal awareness event to a sophisticated cocktail party with the potential to raise thousands of dollars. Regardless, it's important to make sure the organization is clearly represented so that the event becomes the first step of involvement, rather than just a fun event they attended.

Best use? These events are a great and easy way to raise awareness with a group of people likely to support or advocate for your cause.

Media Relations/Public Relations

How would you like free publicity? A few years ago, one of my clients had a front-page article in the local newspaper about their organization.

One of the suggestions in the fundraising / awareness plan we had developed was to hold an event to build partnerships with community members and other organizations serving the same population. In response to a press release about the event, the local paper sent out a reporter who wrote a story that highlighted one of their clients. The day after the article ran, the newspaper included a positive comment on the editorial page about the organization. You can't buy that kind of awareness and credibility. Even if you could, most small organizations wouldn't be able to afford it anyway.

Why did it work? And what are some tips to help you get this kind of awareness?

- o The press release was about something timely and newsworthy.
- o The agency had spent time finding and coaching clients who could speak about their firsthand experiences with the organization.
- o They didn't keep it to themselves.

Don't be afraid of getting out there in a big way. You're doing great work, and people want to hear about it!

Main point? Media relations is a traditional mode of communications that can help to raise awareness with readers of a particular publication.

Financial cost? Unless you hire a PR agency or professional at your organization, the costs are minimal.

Time cost? You'll need to spend time getting to know newspaper editors and writers, as well as the staff at your local TV and radio stations. They are stretched thin, so if you can make their job easier by providing answers to their questions, you could be seen as a good resource, rather than someone who just wants to get their name in the paper. It is essential to find the reporters who cover the geographic and topic area you serve.

Who will you reach? You have the potential to reach anyone who reads the publication the article is published in or listens to the media it is presented on. Many media outlets also offer an online version that you can share through your social media network to help build credibility for your organization.

What format can the message take? You will have little to no control over what is printed. Warning: Nothing said to a journalist is really "off the record."

Best use? Raising awareness and building credibility.

Video

Main point? Video is a very powerful tool to send a clear message about what your organization does and the lives you have impacted. For a good example of a great video, visit CharityWater.com and watch theirs.

Financial cost? It can be expensive to have videos created by a professional as rates are typically around $1,000 per minute. However recording devices have gotten better, and editing software isn't that expensive. It can be fairly simple to create a recorded presentation in PowerPoint and convert it to video format. A video doesn't need to be expensive to be impactful.

Time cost? It is time intensive to develop a video. You will need to outline what you hope to accomplish, write a script, record, and edit your video. While you may choose to hire someone to help with this, you'll have to stay involved to make sure the producer understands your story, what you hope to communicate, and your goal.

Who will you reach? When you post your video online and promote it you have the potential to reach anyone with access to the internet. Since it's not likely that someone would stumble on your video on YouTube, watch it, and then send in a donation, you'll need to find ways to drive people to your videos. You'll also want to make it easy for the viewer to share it with their friends.

What format can the message take? The format of your video can vary from simple PowerPoint presentations with a voiceover to fully edited live footage. While most experts recommend keeping online videos less than two minutes, longer videos have been known to produce good results. Information videos about organizations still tend to be in the five to seven minute range.

Best use? Video can be used to augment and clarify your message. In rare cases, videos can go viral and increase awareness about your organization quickly. However, since it's next to impossible to know which videos will create that kind of energy, it's best to focus on developing an impactful video.

Other

Paid Advertising. With paid advertising, you have complete control over the message you are sending out. This does however often come with a steep price tag. To make the most of your investment you'll want to hire someone who is an expert at ad creation. With this mode of promotion, you have the potential to reach anyone who interacts with the media you are advertising on. The best use for this particular platform is in reaching a specific group of people you know will be interested in what you're doing. This can be done by identifying your ideal donor profile and finding media to advertise on whose readers, viewers, or listeners match that profile.

Phone Calls/Phone Banks. This works well if you have an established group of volunteers or the potential of quickly recruiting callers (as is the case for universities). The cost of a phone bank depends on whether you're using volunteers or a paid company. It is a long-term investment if you're using paid solicitors as first year costs generally exceed income generated. Regardless if you're using volunteers or paid staff, you will need to take the time to prepare scripts. As growing numbers of people choose to opt out of home phone lines it is becoming increasingly difficult to utilize this approach. You can potentially reach anyone for whom you have a current phone number

Closing Thoughts on Communication

Long-term supporters are the lifeblood of successful fundraising programs. So why is it that we so often take our long-term supporters for granted? Think about it for a moment. How absurd would it be if we only called our parents when we wanted money? Or what if you only talked to your boss when you wanted a raise? How long do you think you would keep your job?

Ongoing communication is the key when it comes to building long-term supporters for your organization. Here are three closing thoughts as you are pulling together your communications plan:

Communicate regularly. It might be tempting to try to cut back on messages that you send out. We're all overwhelmed with the amount of information we're processing each day. Our e-mail boxes are overflowing; we have ads popping up all over the Internet; we have RSS feeds that we're following; not to mention Twitter, LinkedIn, and Facebook accounts to try to keep from running us over. It's tempting to cut back—to save other people from that information overload. Cutting back is not the answer. The real answer is to make your communication more meaningful. Make it something they look forward to receiving. Share stories about people your organization is helping. Make it meaningful.

Communicate emotionally. This is where stories become so helpful. Instead of stating, "This makes me sad," share a story that would evoke tears. Let others come to their own conclusions about how they feel. When you read through your materials, pay special attention to assumptions that are made in your writing. As an alternative, provide the backup that led you to that assumption so that readers can make their own assumption as well.

Communicate appropriately. There are so many possibilities for communication these days. The most important thing then is to identify who your most likely supporters are. Once you determine where they look for information, you can select a few different ways to communicate, and build an integrated message. This means (1) communicate where they are, and (2) use different vehicles to reinforce your message.

Key Points to Help You Get Started Quickly

- Be strategic. Know who you're talking to, and communicate appropriately.
- Select just three to five vehicles to start with.
- If you wait until everything is perfect, you'll never get started. The most important thing is to take the first step.

Chapter 6: Winning Foundation Grants
By Betsy Baker

For far too long, many nonprofits have labored under the notion that grant writing is a task similar to filing taxes—something necessary but with as much appeal as a root canal. I think that a lot of this fear and trepidation is often due to the fact that these same nonprofits have not even a clue about how to *begin* writing grants or, if they have written a few (that weren't funded), are ready to give up on the process entirely.

It's not smooth writing that wins grants, although all winning grants follow a process; rather, the winning grant application is a reflection of an organization that is passionate, dedicated, organized, and competent.

This section of *The Essential Fundraising Handbook for Small Nonprofits* is presented to you to make you comfortable with writing grants—and to help you write **successful** applications. I'll share a number of techniques I myself use to do this. I might be one of those rare folks who actually enjoy writing a grant application, but I believe it's because of an understanding of the process (I have been doing this close to twenty years after all!) and employing the same techniques proposal after proposal that results in my enjoyment. So for the next few pages, forget what you think you know about grant writing, and get ready to receive new ideas and information that will have *you* enjoying grant writing—and winning!

First Things First: Get Your House in Order

Let me pose a question to you: Have you ever painted a room? If you'd like your blue room to be yellow, you realize that there is preparation involved in making this happen. Not only do you buy all the equipment such as the paint and the brushes, you spend time taping the room off, sanding off any rough patches, applying a base coat (because yellow paint right on top of blue just isn't going to work), and other prep to result in a smooth, bright, sunny yellow room. As a matter of fact, I'd estimate that time spent on a newly painted room is about 80% in planning and only 20% in actual painting.

The same is true of successful grant applications. Remember when I stated earlier that a winning application isn't just a result of smooth writing? It's the *organization* that the grant maker is funding, not just a well-written proposal.

As a grant writing consultant, I've written many applications on behalf of many different organizations. Awards were always made to those organizations that made sure they were *grant ready*. It wasn't a huge staff, a wildly popular mission, or great connections that made a difference to the grant maker; rather, these winning organizations reflected their passion, dedication, organization, and competence simply by their being. They worked and prepared themselves to become grant ready. Would you like to know what to do to become grant ready? Sure you do, so read on.

The following questions are meant to help ensure that your nonprofit is prepared to submit (and win!) a grant request. Grant funders place a big responsibility on the agency receiving their funds. They want assurance that the organization will be a good steward with the funds that have been entrusted to them.

I recommend gathering your entire staff, board members, and select recipients of your services to answer these questions. Spend time answering each question as completely as possible. To measure your organization's readiness, your answers to this exercise can actually become the "bones" of future proposals. So don't answer the questions just with a *yes* or a *no*. Give descriptive answers. How is something being done? Why is it done this way? You'll see what I mean. This work in the very beginning will do wonders for your applications—not to mention your organization.

How would you answer:

Is your program important?

- Can you demonstrate need for your program? Do you have statistics to prove this need from reputable sources? What would happen if your services went away?
- Can you show significant impact? Do you have evaluation results that prove this impact?
- Does anyone else do what you do? If similar programs exist, what makes you different?

Who does your program affect?

- Can you easily identify your target audience? Describe them in detail.
- Can you demonstrate why this particular target audience should be assisted in some way? What happened in the past that led your organization to begin helping this audience?
- Are there any other target audiences you expect to serve in the future? Why?

Do you present your program well?

- What special accreditations or qualifications allow you to perform your job well?

- Is there a program in place for regular evaluation of staff performance and program success?
- Can you provide third-party endorsements for your efforts such as community awards or complimentary testimonials?
- How do you work to improve your performance?

Does your program make a difference?

- Is your work defined by *benefits* instead of *features*?
- Are you able to demonstrate the difference you make?
- Can you explain why this difference is important?

Is your organization a sound investment?

- Do you have a clearly defined mission?
- Do you have active and qualified staff, board members, advisors, and volunteers?
- Can you prove that your approach follows the best practice in your field?
- Does your governing body understand its appropriate role?
- Are your bylaws effective and up-to-date?
- Is there a personnel policy and ethics statement in place?

- Is a financial management plan in place (including an annual audit and an investment plan)?
- Can your program be easily replicated in other communities?

Are you a good funding partner?

- Is there a system in place to thank grant partners?
- Do you have the ability to manage the project for which you have received funding?
- Do you submit required reports on time?
- Do you live up to any advertising you have promised a grantor?
- Can you demonstrate other successful partnerships with granting agencies or other nonprofit agencies with a similar mission?
- Have you been responsible with funding so that the funder will want to partner with you again in the future?

I picture you (along with staff, board members, and beneficences) in a large room taking a day or two to really hash out these topics and work together to improve your performance in the community. See how the preparation for a grant application really has everything to do with your preparation as an organization?

Why Should You Care About Getting a Grant Anyway?

Okay, so I never said that getting grants was easy. Why is it so important to go to all of this trouble? I'm glad you asked.

Organizations that have received grants are well respected. R-E-S-P-E-C-T. This is what you receive from other potential donors to your organization when you tell them you've won a hard-earned grant. They immediately understand that your financial house is in order since all of your financials have been on display to the grantor, that your staff is well-equipped and competent (since they're expected to perform the duties outlined in the grant), and that your organization has proved itself in competition to be better than other applicants. You know how in certain places you can drop a name and get special attention based on that connection? The same is true when you mention to a potential major gift donor or special event underwriter that you have received funding from a prominent grantor. It can give you "instant cache" in their eyes. You have already proven yourself worthy of funding.

Grant funding can also mean a huge transformation for your nonprofit. One regional hospital foundation I worked for received a grant that allowed the number of school nurses in one county to increase from one to three, covering all the schools in that system. This was an emotional achievement because a child had died at one of the schools simply because the nurse wasn't present at the school that day. Now each school could have its very own nurse. It can literally take years of special events to match the income that one grant can bring into an organization.

Did you know too that billions of dollars are given each year in grant funding? Just like the lottery, you have to be in it to win it! Unlike winning the lottery though, your chances are much, much better. The Giving USA Foundation reports that each year, corporations and private foundations award nonprofits upward of $50 billion—this figure doesn't even include government grant money! Big nonprofits, little nonprofits, well-connected, zero connections—the playing field is level. Again, it comes down to the passion, dedication, organization, and competence of the nonprofit. So let's talk next about how to get these things across in your application.

How Well Do You Tell Your Nonprofit's Story?

In an earlier chapter, Lori Jacobwith shared with us how to find and share stories. This is important for grants as well.

From the beginning of time, people have communicated their ideas, values, and lessons through stories. Imagine friends and family sitting around a fire telling stories. Stories later were depicted through cave drawings, and then eventually, written forms of language were developed to tell stories.

Corporations rely on storytelling every day to sell their products. How often do you see commercials that feature "real people" who have lost fifty pounds? Some nonprofits have also been hugely successful in using storytelling to raise significant amounts of money. Charity: water, which provides access to clean water, is such an example.

For her ninth birthday, Rachel Beckwith wanted to raise $300 for charity: water. In the month after her birthday, she had raised $220. Not long after, Rachel was in a fatal car accident. News about her commitment to the charity spread, and in less than three months after her death, nearly thirty-two thousand people had donated $1.2 million to charity: water in her name. Although it's a sad story, this is just one example of how nonprofits use storytelling to promote good causes.

It's my guess that you've never thought of a grant application as an opportunity for storytelling. After all, you're confined by page limits, answering only certain questions and having to come up with such things as goals and objectives and evaluation methods. It sounds dreadful.

But just as a good story provides a hook to make the reader want to read more, nonprofits have this same necessity to engage their audience with the first sentence. It's easier to do this when you think of your nonprofit's story just like a good book with characters, a plot, and a setting.

Know your nonprofit's story inside and out. The best way to do this is to get out of your office and into the field to see and experience the actual work that your agency does. At one time, I consulted with a nonprofit that provided assistance to cancer patients who had no financial means to get the treatment their doctor prescribed. The agency met with prospective clients, enrolled them in the program, and then provided gasoline vouchers to help get them to their chemotherapy and radiation appointments. Some clients lived in rural areas, were miles away from the treatment facility, and had been prescribed five treatments per week for eight weeks. That's forty round-trips! The agency's other main assistance program was provision of access to often expensive prescription medications.

This nonprofit's staff consisted of an executive director, an administrative assistant, a social worker, and a medication coordinator. While I spent plenty of time with the executive director, it wasn't until I spent time with the program staff and the clients that I had a full understanding of what the organization was doing and how important it was in the community. Nothing can take the place of a personal experience.

I encourage you to get to know and understand your organization intimately by spending time to do the same. Get to know and understand your organization, spending time in the field. In addition to firsthand observation, collect anecdotes from program staff and clients, and begin keeping a file of testimonials. They help add color to your writing and help you flesh out your characters, plot, and setting in your story.

Your Organization's Need

If we were to think of writing a grant proposal like building a house, adding one thing at a time, the need that you describe in your proposal would be the actual framework of the house. Without a strong *needs statement,* your proposal will collapse onto itself. Here are a few tips to help you develop your needs statement:

First, recognize that all needs should be external to the organization. In other words, they need to be of benefit to the public you serve. Yes, an iPad may be something that **you** want, but unless you can find a way to justify your target audience benefiting, leave that on your own personal wish list. Grant makers aren't Santa Claus.

Let's imagine though that your organization desires a new building on your school's campus. Instead of making it about the **organization** needing a new building, focus on the **students** needing a new building. What would a new building mean to your students? A new building means you can add more classes. More classes mean that more students learn the skills they need to get jobs. Is an uneducated workforce your challenge? Then you just presented a need and offered a compelling solution.

Second, lead with need. Before you begin describing the project you want to have funded, present your compelling need. Think about crafting your proposal as you would an elevator speech. When you lead with need, it gets the grant reviewer's attention. Remember, a need is simply a condition or situation in which something is required. Present your need first and your conditions to meet those needs next.

Third, present need with concrete evidence. Even though the problem is evident to your organization, a grant funder needs more than you telling them that there's a problem—it has to be shown. National data is helpful, but the closer you drill down to your local area, the better. Describe your need so that it paints a picture inside of the reviewer's head. Try county census data, county health profiles (usually found on your state's public health department's website), quotes from recognized area subject experts, and other published reports.

Expect that the grant reviewers won't know the people you serve as intimately as you do. Make it as easy on them as possible to get to know your audience better. Remember that grant funders are looking for a social return on their investment, and they invest in people they feel they know.

Fourth, avoid mistakes. Here are the most common ones I see: a complicated need, confusing the solution with the problem, using adjectives instead of compelling details, too much focus on an organization's needs, too little documentation that a problem exists, needs that don't align with the organization. I could go on but I'll spare you. Do you see how each of these mistakes could be seen in a grant reviewer's eyes? We have to prepare our proposals precisely and be dedicated to introducing the grant funder fully to our audience and their need. When the funder "gets" the need, and is moved by it, money follows.

How to Find Grants for Your Nonprofit/How to Understand Grant Funder's Guidelines

You are better equipped now to tell your nonprofit's story in a compelling way as well as to present your need. Next, you need to find the right funders.

One common challenge that all grant writers have is finding funders whose missions match that of their nonprofit. There are literally thousands of grant-funding institutions, so be prepared to spend many hours searching for those that are a good match. There's really no easy way around this. Let me share with you what I do to make the process less challenging.

First, find a *similar* nonprofit to yours, locate their funders (on the website's donor page or annual report), and start investigating those for your own nonprofit. I'll explain what I mean.

Let's say, for example, that the nonprofit you're working with is a not-for-profit hospital foundation. The hospital foundation is broadly centered on community health, preventative health measures, and patient care. We'll call our nonprofit the ABC Hospital Foundation. Before we begin investigating grant makers for the ABC Foundation, let's visit the website of the XYZ Foundation, which also happens to be a not-for-profit hospital foundation in the same local community. There we find a donor page, which lists the individuals and grant makers who have financially supported them. You'll want to make a list of these grant makers.

Next, as it pertains to your nonprofit, come up with a list of key words in starting your research, including subject area (such as *health* or *environment*), geographic area (such as *Boston* or *Massachusetts*), and target population information such as race, gender, and socioeconomic status (such as *Latino women living below federal poverty guidelines*). Doing so will refine and target your search.

Once you have your list of possible funding sources plus your targeted search criteria, you can begin your investigation on grant maker's websites and on the Foundation Center's website.

Please note: Your investigation shouldn't stop at competing nonprofits! This is simply meant as a suggestion for a starting point. Continue to dig using the following sources.

Using the Foundation Center Website

The first place I go to for grant maker research is the Foundation Center (www.FoundationCenter.org), especially if I have no information (not even a website name) for the funder I'm curious about. This is how the Foundation Center describes itself:

"Established in 1956, the Foundation Center is the leading source of information about philanthropy worldwide. Through data, analysis, and training, we connect people who want to change the world to the resources they need to succeed. The center maintains the most comprehensive database on U.S. and, increasingly, global grant makers and their grants—a robust, accessible knowledge bank for the sector."

I am not a paid endorser for the Foundation Center. I just find that, with information on tens of thousands of grant makers, they are the most useful source for finding information on grant-making foundations, and much of their information is FREE.

Using the Foundation Center Website for FREE

To investigate for FREE grant-making foundations you think would be good matches for your nonprofit, simply go to the Foundation Center's home page. You'll see a section just for Grant Seekers with a search box where you can type in the name of the funder. Information about the funder will appear such as contact information, the employer ID number (EIN), basic financial data, and, if available, the funder's website address.

It is also interesting to check out the grant maker's 990-PF, which is also available on the Foundation Center website. All grant-making foundations, in compliance with the IRS, have to submit this form, and it's public information. You'll find more detailed financial information such as assets, expenditures, and a list of past grant recipients with award amounts. This last piece is critical information because it's important to know the range of funding to request. The

990 is a basic but powerful tool in finding grant makers who give to organizations such as yours.

Using a Grant Maker's Website

The ultimate destination in your search for possible grant funders is the funder's website.

Getting to know a grant maker is critical in the success of winning a grant from them. Many make their annual reports available online, providing a great place to see what is important to them. They'll also post individual project success stories—again, indicating what they value. Are the projects they fund similar to the one you want funding for? You can also find out staff names and what program officers are in charge of different funding divisions.

The most important information you'll find will be application and submission guidelines for the foundation. Using the nonprofit hospital foundation example, if your ABC Hospital Foundation is located in Tennessee, and the funder only funds in the states of Florida and Alabama, they won't be a good match.

All of these research tools work together. It just takes practice to learn what works best for you.

Other websites for you to check out that list of grant funders by location and by area of interest:

- The Foundation Center produces the RFP Bulletin sends grant opportunities right to your inbox! Register at http://foundationcenter.org/ to begin receiving them.
- Www.Nozasearch.com provides grant activity updates.
- Chronicle of Philanthropy at www.philanthropy.com. Fundraising tab → New Grants.
- The Grantsmanship Center at www.TGCI.com. Funding Sources tab → Funding State-by-State.
- Www.FundsNetServices.com. Funding by category.

If you're not finding what you want with these free services, the Foundation Center has a paid subscription service called *Foundation Directory Online*. You can usually get a free thirty-day pass to try it. I highly recommend it— it's what I use in addition to the free sites listed above. Call them directly to see which service could be tailored just for you.

Understanding Grant Funder's Guidelines

As you're investigating grantors that appear to fit your agency's purpose, mission, or program, you will also want to be aware of funding criteria such as:

Eligibility – Does the funder accept unsolicited grant applications or give only to preselected organizations? Do they only consider applications from a certain city, region, or state? Don't waste time with a funder that plainly states they do not accept applications outside a specific area or only focus on a certain region of the country that your organization is not in.

Foundation's Purpose – Foundations exist to fund organizations that have matching goals and interests as their own. For example, if their interest lies in feeding the hungry in Africa, they are not likely to support an inner-city children's ballet program.

Funding Restrictions – Funders sometimes put restrictions in the project budget regarding the use of the funds or can even require that their grant must be matched dollar for dollar with other monies or in-kind services.

What the Foundation Funds – The funder will specify their area of interest. For example, they might be committed to the prevention of teen pregnancy, early childhood education programs, or health information technology. If your area of interest isn't at least broadly mentioned, e.g., "health care," which can encompass many different interests within the area of health, don't bother.

What the Foundation Does Not Fund – Funders will sometimes specify if they won't pay for a certain line item in your project budget. For example, they may not pay for an existing program's operating costs, a capital campaign, advertising, etc. All of these line items may be included in the overall project budget. Just don't expect their grant money to be used for these purposes.

You can find many great opportunities through your research, and it's easy to get lost in all of your possibilities. Be sure to organize your information so you can keep up with the different stages of your proposal. There are a number of software programs on the market today to track grant-funding prospects—a couple that have gotten good reviews include GrantWave[11] and AmpliFund.[12]

Writing the Application

Once you've identified grant-funding prospects and begin writing their applications, I think that you'll find most applications follow a similar format. Here are the most common things you'll find they want:

A compelling need for your organization's project. As I stated earlier, this is the framework for your entire proposal. It has to be convincing and make your funder want to support it. Of course, it should also have a clear relationship to your organization's mission and purpose. Remember, you always want your need to describe your client's needs—not your needs as an organization.

Clear goals and objectives. Once you establish the need, you have to be able to explain how your program is going to meet that need (goals and objectives identify that). Goals define what the organization is trying to accomplish through its project. Objectives are activities that measure the success of the organization's progress toward those

---

[11] http://mindcoast.com/
[12] http://streamlinksoftware.com/products/amplifund

goals. We'll be discussing the difference between goals and objectives later in this chapter.

Evaluation of your project. Funders like to see that you have a built-in component for measuring the success of your project. Evaluation is intended to answer questions such as:

- What impact did our program have on the intended audience?
- What changed as a result of our project?
- What was the most appreciated result?
- What could we have done differently?

You want the audience to benefit, and you need to know what to change, if anything, if the intended results aren't met.

Project sustainability. Funders want to know how you'll be continuing your project after their grant investment is gone. And it will come to an end one day. This is where you define your plan for continuing the project by means other than the grant maker. This might include writing applications to other grant makers, an individual giving campaign, or special fundraising events. It just shows that you're committed to a variety of fundraising techniques, and that you aren't solely dependent on this one grant funder's investment.

A project budget estimating income and expenses. Most simply, the budget is the financial picture of your program. The best budgets directly translate the strategies and methods section of your proposal into dollar amounts—words into numbers is another way of describing it.

These are the most common sections of a grant proposal. Let's dive a little further into a couple of the more complicated of these sections. These sections are the two I'm most often asked about—how to write goals and objectives and how to write an evaluation plan. Now you'll know too!

Goals and Objectives of a Grant Application

The purpose of this section in the application is to answer "So, what?" You've identified a need in the community. Your goals and objectives will describe, "So here's what we're proposing to meet this need." Remember how we defined goals and objectives. A goal is described as what the nonprofit is trying to accomplish. An objective is something measurable that the nonprofit does to try and meet that goal. It measures success in meeting the goal.

Here are some ways to distinguish between goals and objectives:

- Goals are broad. Objectives are narrow.
- Goals are abstract. Objectives are concrete.
- Goals are intangible—something you can't put your hands on. Objectives are tangible—they're something you can reach.
- Finally, goals are mainly general intentions while objectives are very precise intentions.

Let me give you a few more guidelines just on writing objectives since they are more specific:

- Objectives should always be stated in quantifiable terms.
- They should also be stated in terms of outcomes.
- You also have to be realistic with objectives and not reach for completing them in an unrealistic time frame. Remember, you usually have a whole year (or more) to complete your project in a funder's

time line. Giving the organization unrealistic objectives sends a red flag to funders. They know that your agency isn't superhuman.

Let me give you a real-life example of a goal and an objective.

One of my clients is a cancer wellness foundation. The overall goal of this foundation is to serve cancer patients who can't afford treatment. Here is how I've stated their goal in grant applications:

To provide comprehensive access to care to cancer patients in Central Alabama, including the indigent, underinsured, and uninsured patients who cannot afford comprehensive care as prescribed by their doctor.

The main services they provide are transportation to and from radiation and chemo appointments because a lot of patients live in rural areas and lack reliable transportation. The foundation raises money to pay for taxi and bus trips to get the patients to their treatment.

Because this service supports the foundation's goal, I worded the objective for my grant applications like this:

To increase access to transportation to chemo and radiation appointments for at least one thousand indigent, underinsured, and uninsured cancer patients within one year.

See how my goal is very general but my objective is very precise? A good rule of thumb to follow in writing objectives is to include a direction of change, an area of change, who the target population is that will be impacted, the degree of change, and the time frame.

So in the objective, I just gave you:

- direction of change
- to increase
- area of change
- transportation opportunities
- target population impacted
- underserved cancer patients
- degree of change
- at least one thousand patients
- time frame,
- within one year

Let's wrap all of this information up here with an example:

Goals and Objectives Example

Goal:

To provide comprehensive access to care to cancer patients in Central Alabama, including the indigent, underinsured, and uninsured patients who cannot afford comprehensive care as prescribed by their doctor.

	Objective 1	**Objective 2**
Direction of Change	Increase	Increase
Area of Change	Access to transportation to chemo and radiation appointments	Access to prescribed cancer medications
Target Population	Indigent, underinsured, and uninsured cancer patients	Indigent, underinsured, and uninsured cancer patients
Degree of Change	A minimum of one thousand individuals served	A minimum of one thousand individuals served
Time Frame	One year	One year

One of the objectives to support the above goal would then be stated this way:

To increase access to transportation to chemo and radiation appointments for at least one thousand indigent, underinsured, and uninsured cancer patients within one year.

Objectives are usually meant to reduce something, to increase something, to decrease something, or to expand something.

Always have the end in mind when writing goals and objectives. Answering these five questions will help get you started every time:

- What is the key focus that your organization is seeking to change?
- What segment of the population will be affected by the change?
- What direction of change (increase, decrease, expand, or reduce) is your organization seeking to enable?
- What is the extent of change your organization hopes to make?
- What is the deadline for enacting that change?

Using the above questions will help you get started. Once they're written, ask yourself these review questions:

1. Is (are) your goal(s) stated as a result of what you want accomplished?
2. Are the objectives related to your goal and stated specifically?
3. Can the progress of your project be measured according to quantifiable assessments?
4. Is the target population easily identifiable, and does the project have clear time lines?

Develop the Evaluation Component

Evaluation measures the effectiveness of the grant program for which you received funding. Grant funders like to see an evaluation method in place before a grant is given because they want to see a measure of return on their investment.

Good evaluation measures the impact that a program is having on the community, its effectiveness, and its efficiency. It should reveal what worked in the program and—equally important—what didn't work so that it helps improve the program in the future.

Specifically, good evaluation helps strengthen your proposal's chances for funding. A foundation likes to see that you're taking their investment seriously, and that if you find any flaws in your program through evaluation, that you'll address those. It assures the foundation that you're interested in delivering the best program possible in the community.

Evaluation also helps your organization learn about its strengths and weaknesses. Just the process of thinking through an evaluation design can strengthen a program before it's ever introduced. And this design also helps correct issues **as** the project is being delivered.

Another benefit is being able to report good feedback on your program to current funders and to future funders. Evaluation verifies and documents that you're making progress in the community. Funders like to see concrete evidence.

Here are six different ideas about **how** to implement evaluation of an organization's grant project. You can use *project participant questionnaires, data review, group observation, one-on-one interviews, focus groups, and case studies.*

For the sake of example, let's assume that your proposed project is designed to reduce childhood obesity through a school health program. This is how you could use the tools I just mentioned to measure the success of the project.

First, let's talk about how you'd use **participant questionnaires**—if you chose this method of measure, you'd simply be asking participants a list of set questions before you introduce the program and after to measure the benefit the program is having. In this instance, you would want to administer a behavior survey before participation, and then offer the same survey at the end of the program to see if attitudes have changed. A question you might ask in this example is "How many minutes a day are you exercising?" You'd hope to see an increase in the number of minutes per day at the end of your program.

Data review is simply recording measurable factors. In the case of our example, measurable data would include body weight and body mass index. You could measure this both before the program and after.

Another form of evaluation is **observation**. Without letting participants know, you can observe and monitor behavior. In our example, this might include recording how many kids actually participated in physical activity during outside breaks—how long they stayed active and also observing how many kids didn't engage in physical activity.

One-on-one interviews are another great form of evaluation. Sit down with participants one-on-one, and get as much information from them as you can. This is a little different from a written survey because you have the opportunity to ask additional questions and get additional information from them. You can also ask them to offer constructive criticism of the program.

Focus groups are another popular form of evaluation. These are similar to interviews, but the participants are in a group and can hear one another's responses. This type of evaluation can have both a positive and a negative influence on responses. Positive in that it can encourage interactive discussion, prompting lots of opinions, or negative in that participants don't necessarily want their views known in front of others.

Last, let's discuss **case studies**. This is where you follow an individual participant and record minute details about changes that occurred in his or her life as a result of your program. Imagine what a compelling personal story it would be if you took a child with a history of family obesity, juvenile diabetes, and no knowledge of healthy habits and, at the end of your program, had a child who had lost weight, made healthier food choices, and found that he/she loved sports. While case studies are never an indicator of how your program changed lives overall, they can be convincing that you are indeed changing certain lives.

So which evaluation method is best? That's up to you and your organization to decide. When you're preparing the evaluation, your answers to the following questions will help frame your evaluation:

1. What's the purpose of your organization's evaluation?
2. How will your findings be used?
3. What will you know after the evaluation that you won't know before?
4. How has the community been positively impacted as a result of your program?

You can use these **questions** to frame the evaluation portion of your grant application (sample answers are in italics):

1. What kind of data will you be collecting?

   --At what points?

   --Using what methods of collection?

   Numbers of kids participating in the eight-week healthy habits curriculum course.

   --Once a week for eight weeks.

   --Preprogram and post program questionnaires.

2. If you use a sample of participants, how will they be selected?

   With the help of teachers who have identified students with poor health habits.

3. What measurement will you use to determine if the program was implemented as planned?

   Notes detailing days and times that the curriculum was followed.

4. Who is responsible for conducting the evaluation?

   Assigned staff working with the physical education teacher responsible for introducing the curriculum.

5. Who will receive results of the evaluation?

   Staff, board, funding partners, community.

6. How will you define success for the program?

   Meeting or exceeding program objectives.

Conclusion

I hope that you've found this guide both informative and motivating. It's a lot of information to process, isn't it? Don't let it overload your brain—keep things in perspective. Even though you're not going to win a financial reward for every grant application you write, you will receive a personal reward by refining your process with each grant application written. The next grant is always going to be written a bit better than the previous one.

Persistence is the name of the game, and knowing you have the ability to make your community a better place with just the stroke of your pen (or your keyboard) is a great motivator!

Also, if you have found this book helpful and fun, you might want to check out some of my online training opportunities for you at www.YourGrantAuthority.com under the Products tab.

Chapter 7: Special Events Overview
By Sandy Rees

Special events have an important place in a good overall fundraising program. One or maybe two well-done special events can generate publicity for your organization in addition to raising money. Events can also give you a way to cultivate relationships.

You should have one signature event that brings you lots of community awareness, leverages media sponsors, and raises money. Do no more than two special events each year. I suggest that you try to get corporate sponsors for your events if you can. Businesses and corporations are usually looking for exposure and goodwill for their dollars, and this is a good way to give them that.

Be very careful not to get on the "special event hamster wheel" where you are holding too many events during the year. This is not the best use of your time and will not bring you the results you want. You might spend all your time working on events that bring in only a few hundred dollars instead of working on things that can bring in much more money.

Purpose

Clarity will help you hold a successful event. The clearer you are about the event's purpose, the event's audience, and the results you want, the more likely you'll be satisfied with the results from your event.

The very first thing you should get clear about is the purpose of the event.

Knowing your purpose will help you set the direction and expectations for the event to ensure success. It will also help you narrow down the list of donors or potential donors you invite to the event so that you are getting the people who will help you meet your expectations and goals for the event.

Every event you hold should do one or more of these four things for you:

- **Raise money.** You should generate enough money from the event that it was clearly worth the time and energy to hold the event.
- **Raise awareness.** You should get plenty of publicity and exposure with your event.

- **Deepen relationships.** Your event should give you the chance to enhance relationships with donors, sponsors, and volunteers.
- **Bring in additional resources.** Your event should bring in additional resources like supplies or in-kind donations.

Every event you hold should bring more prospects to the table too. Be sure to plan a way to connect with those prospects so you can communicate with them later.

Sponsors

Most events make their money through sponsorships. If your event garners publicity, particularly through the media, you can probably secure at least one corporate sponsor. Good candidates for sponsors are banks, communications companies, and other businesses that have broad target audiences. However, the best way to decide on a corporate sponsor is to first consider the audience that the event will attract; then find businesses who are after that same target audience. They'll be the most likely to say yes to a sponsorship.

Keep in mind that the more the sponsor will get from their experience, the more money they'll be willing to pay. Be prepared to outline all the benefits the sponsor will receive, including exposure of their name and logo, association with a great charity, opportunity to get in front of their target audience, etc.

Volunteers

Volunteers are often the backbone of a successful event. From planning to execution, those extra hands make a big difference!

Start by recruiting volunteers to help you plan and execute your event. You can get help pulling the event off, and you will probably get some good ideas too. Plus, involving volunteers in the work you are doing is a great way to get to know them and build a relationship. After all, it's all about relationships!

Planning

Once you set the date for your event, use a time line to back up from the event to plan all the details. You can include things like sending a press release to the local media a week before the event, confirming with a caterer two days before the event, and so forth. This great planning tool can help you keep track of all the details and avoid letting things fall between the cracks.

Lessons Learned

After the event, have a meeting with your planning committee and any other people involved to have a "lessons learned" session. Talk about what went well and what didn't. Make notes about each item you discuss, and save the notes for your first planning meeting next year. That gives you something to start from next year and, hopefully, avoid repeating any mistakes.

Maximize Attendance

Getting people to attend your special event can be a challenge, particularly if your organization is small and relatively unknown. Here are a few tips for filling your event.

1. **Have a fun and unique event.** The more interesting and appealing your event sounds, the more likely

people will want to come. If your event is different from all the others in your community, that will also help draw guests in.

2. **Recruit media sponsors to help publicize your event.** Having media attention for your event will not only help get the word out in the community, but also give your event a bit of credibility. After all, radio and television stations wouldn't talk about it if it wasn't going to be a good event, right?

3. **Have a local celebrity as a spokesperson.** If you have a local celebrity who is willing to be a spokesperson for your event, that will also encourage people to attend. And if guests have the chance to meet and mingle with the celebrity at the event, even better!

4. **Sell corporate tables or teams.** Businesses are usually willing to purchase a whole table or team full of tickets and then give them to their employees as a benefit. This is a great way to get new people exposed to your organization and fill a table or team at the same time.

5. **Recruit table captains or team captains.** For some events, table or team captains can be the best way to get new faces to attend. Table or team captains typically are people who are friends of your organization and who recruit their friends to fill a table.

6. **Send invitations to your supporters.** Don't overlook the obvious! Invite your current donors and volunteers to the event.

Spend some time thinking about the special events you plan to hold during the coming year. For each one, use the Special Event Success Checklist to help you complete each task. Use the remaining special event worksheets to help you make your event a success.

Special Event Success Checklist

Event name: _____

Event date: _____

☐ Event's purpose is clearly defined (friendraiser, fundraiser, publicity, etc.).

☐ Target audience for event attendees is clearly defined.

☐ Event is unique.

☐ Goals for the event have been set.

☐ An event budget has been created.

☐ Promotion plan for the event has been created and implemented.

☐ Planning committee has been created, involving a combination of staff, board, and volunteers.

☐ Date for the event has been chosen that doesn't conflict with any other significant community activities.

☐ Venue for the event has been chosen and confirmed.

☐ Corporate sponsors have been solicited.

☐ Media sponsors have been solicited.

☐ List of volunteer roles that need to be filled for the event has been created.

☐ Roles for board and staff during the event have been clearly defined.

☐ "Lessons learned" meeting has been planned to gather information after the event.

☐ _____

☐ _____

Special Event Budget Worksheet

Event: _____

Event date: _____

Revenue

Corporate Sponsorships	$_____
Ticket Sales	$_____
Donations	$_____
Silent Auction	$_____
Other	$_____

Total Revenue　　　　$_____

Expenses

Event Location Rental	$_____
Food	$_____
Entertainment	$_____
Equipment Rental	$_____
Decorations	$_____
Graphic Design	$_____
Printing	$_____
Postage	$_____
Other	$_____

Total Expenses　　　　$_____

Special Event Planning Checklist

Seven to twelve months ahead:

☐ Decide event purpose (raise funds, raise awareness, acquire supporters, etc.).

☐ Choose event date.

☐ Choose event type (dinner, party, etc.).

☐ Choose event theme.

☐ Research possible event sites.

☐ Get cost estimates (food, site rental, entertainment, etc.).

☐ Create event budget.

☐ Decide on ticket price.

☐ Create sponsorship levels.

☐ Recruit sponsors.

Six months ahead:

☐ Book event site.

☐ Book entertainment.

☐ Recruit event chairperson(s).

☐ Assist in recruiting committee members.

☐ Recruit media sponsors.

Three to six months ahead:

☐ Hold regular committee meetings.

☐ Create save-the-date card and/or invitation.

☐ Have save-the-date card and/or invitation printed.

☐ Investigate need for special permits, licenses, insurance, etc.

☐ Request logos from corporate sponsors for printing.

Ten to twelve weeks ahead:

☐ Compile mailing list.

☐ Mail save-the-date card.

☐ Confirm menu with event site/caterer.

Six weeks ahead:

☐ Mail invitations.

☐ Order awards (if appropriate).

Two weeks ahead:

☐ Create "day of event" assignment task lists for volunteers.

☐ Confirm entertainment.

☐ Schedule deliveries of special equipment/rentals.

☐ Create seating chart.

☐ Arrange for pickup/return of special equipment/rentals.

☐ Write and distribute press release to local media.

☐ Recruit someone to serve as event photographer.

One week ahead:

☐ Begin gathering supplies needed for day of event (cash box, credit card slips, pens, notepads, paper clips, stapler, tape, etc.)

☐ Confirm setup/teardown with event site.

☐ Confirm meal count with caterer (confirm any vegetarian or special request dishes).

☐ Meet with committee on last-minute details.

☐ Finalize registration.

☐ Make follow-up calls to media.

☐ Write checks for payments to be made on the day of the event.

☐ Prepare name tags (if necessary).

Day before:

☐ Final walk-through of event site.

☐ Recheck all supplies needed for the event.

Day of event:

☐ Arrive early.

☐ Set up registration.

☐ Sound/light check.

Week after event:

☐ Hold "lessons learned" meeting with committee.

Special Event Lessons Learned Worksheet

After each special event, you should gather the committee members who worked on the event, staff and volunteers who participated, and other key people together to debrief them. The only way you can make the event even better next year is to uncover what needs improvement. Don't trust your opinion to be the only important one; you need to hear from a variety of people about what worked and what didn't.

Special event name: _____

_____

Special event date: _____

      Dollars raised: $_____

Did the event accomplish its purpose? _____

_____

_____

_____

_____

_____

What went well with the event? _____

_____

_____

_____

_____

_____

_____

What needs to be improved next year if this event is

held again?_____

_____

_____

_____

_____

_____

_____

What was the overall response of the event attendees?

Did they seem to enjoy themselves?_____

_____

_____

_____

Should this event be held again? Why or why not?_____

_____

_____

_____

_____

Chapter 8: Fine-Tuning a Silent Auction for Greater Revenue

By Sherry Truhlar, CMP, BAS, CAI

Silent auctions have grown in popularity as nonprofits seek ways to get more mileage out of their fundraising events.

Perhaps it's because a silent auction doesn't require a commitment of focused time, like a live auction does. Silent auctions often run concurrently during other scheduled activities, such as a reception or dinner. They are also easier to legally administer than a raffle, which might mandate a state license.

Another advantage of the silent auction is that you may not need to work in the procurement trenches, securing items. Unlike other methods of fundraising (direct asks, capital campaigns), you (the nonprofit staff) don't necessarily need to be the one "doing" the project. A number of my clients outsource procurement to volunteers or interns. Though you wouldn't dream of asking an intern to visit a donor and request a $10,000 gift, you *would* ask an intern to walk down Main Street, USA, (or surf the Internet) and request a $100 donation from a store.

About Sherry

During an economic tailspin, I substituted for a friend at a workshop called "Managing Your Career in Turbulent Times." The class was designed for MBAs (of which I wasn't) who had graduated from Georgetown, Harvard, or Wharton business schools (of which I hadn't). No one bothered to check diplomas at the door, so I slipped into an empty seat. "Life rarely moves in a linear fashion," the instructor said and proceeded to explain how the path to your dream job is never a straight line.

That simple statement explains how I so perfectly and yet so unpredictably started my own benefit auction firm in 2005. A random decision to attend auctioneer school to learn to "talk fast" (we auctioneers call it "the chant") led me to leave GE, taking everything I'd learned about planning profitable corporate events and applying it to my new field of fundraising auction galas.

Yet, that's only half the story.

Long before that, I grew up in a family where work was a big part of our lives. My parents held two jobs (working for companies, in addition to having their own entrepreneurial ventures), so laziness wasn't something witnessed. And for nearly all of my life, I've held at least two distinctly different jobs, mimicking what I saw as a child. For instance, when I launched Red Apple Auctions, I balanced it with bookings in Europe and the USA modeling as a plus-size fashion model, managing a rental property, and serving as the marketing coordinator of a small church!

Here's what I know: Whatever your position or industry, you'll best be served in life when you have the confidence to articulate what you offer. Whether it's finding a great spouse, getting a raise, buying a car, or convincing a stranger to make a donation to your nonprofit, you've got to know how to present your case to accomplish your goal. And once you know the process, it's not that hard. It's certainly not brain surgery.

So that's the crux of what I now do. I've taught thousands of auction planners—volunteers and professionals—how to improve their benefit auction fundraisers so they raise thousands upon thousands more dollars. And it's nothing more than teaching them the same marketing and sales skills I've honed through my work in dozens of industries, starting at age fourteen. You can learn more at www.RedAppleAuctions.com.

And as procurement is usually the most time-consuming element of an auction, it's useful to get this off your to-do list and into the hands of others.

But for all these perks, silent auctions have a big limitation. Historically, they haven't been big moneymakers.

It varies by item, but national averages for yields of silent auctions fall into the 50% to 65% range. That means for every $1.00 worth of value offered in the silent auction, it generates .50 to .65 cents. Once you consider the time involved in procuring and marketing the items, one may wonder if this is a wise fundraising approach.

There is good news. **When you get the right items with the right crowd and market them well, silent auction yields improve.**

Using the tips you're about to learn (and other strategies), my clients have watched yields increase. One client surpassed 100% yields, which is generally what we'd expect only from a live auction sale! To put that another way, for every dollar's worth of value on the silent auction table, she sold it for *more* than that. More realistically, aim for smaller improvements of a 5–10% gain from your existing yield.

Before we dive in, it will be helpful to offer some guidelines for planning silent auctions.

Guideline Number 1: Set a goal.
As already mentioned, national averages show that a silent auction will make between .50 and .65 cents on the dollar. Although I'd encourage you to analyze your own silent auction and use that data when conducting this exercise, let's work from the national statistics as an example.

If your goal is to raise $10,000 in a silent auction, you're going to need (using national averages) to procure $15,384 (at 65% of value) to $20,000 (at 50% of value) worth of items.

Guideline Number 2: Restrict the number of items.
One of the most common mistakes of silent auctions is that the committee offers too many items.

Auctions are based on scarcity. We want lots of bidders competing for a few items. When you mess up the scarcity factor, your auction yields decline, regardless of how great the items are or how well you market them.

So how many silent auction items is the *right* number for your event? The goal is to have an average of two bidders per silent auction package.

A simple formula is as follows.

> Number of guests / 2 = Number of buying units
> Number of buying units / 2 = Targeted number of silent auction packages

For example, a social services client runs a Friday night gala for five hundred guests. The attendees sit at sponsored tables and usually come with their spouse. This represents two people per wallet, so the targeted number of silent auction packages would be 125.

> 500 guests / 2 = 250 buying units
> 250 buying units / 2 = 125 targeted number of silent auction packages

Another client runs a Thursday luncheon that attracts about 120 women. These women purchase their own tickets and rarely bring a spouse or guest. For this event, the targeted number of silent auction packages would be sixty.

> 120 buying units / 2 = 60 targeted number of silent auction packages

Confused? Just think of it this way. If your room will be filled with couples, you'll be dividing by *two* twice because couples usually share expenses. But if your room will be filled with singles, you'll divide by *two* once because singles are responsible for their own expenses.

The bottom line is that we want two buying units (be that a single person or a couple) per silent auction package.

Reducing the number of items might feel uncomfortable. It might go against what seems logical. Yet one of my clients reduced her silent auction by one hundred items and raised the same amount of money as she had the previous year. That meant a lot less work for her and her committee!

Guideline Number 3: Use these data points to target your average package value.
Now we need to figure out what value of item should be on the table to reach our goal.

If our goal is to raise $10,000, and we have five hundred couples attending, our average silent auction item value will need to be between $123 and $160. Here's how we know that.

First, determine the number of packages you need.
- 500 guests / 2 = 250 buying units
- 250 buying units / 2 = 125 maximum targeted number of auction packages

Then we take our procured valued and divide by the maximum number of packages.

- $20,000 procured value / 125 auction packages = $160 average package value
- $15,384 procured value / 125 auction packages = $123 average package value

As you procure and package items, use this information to be strategic. For example, if you collect a $25 gift card from a salon, you'll need to combine that with a few things to reach a $123 to $160 package value for your table. And if you collect a $300 gift card to a top restaurant, that's the equivalent of about two items. You might want to scale back and only offer 124 packages.

Guideline Number 4: Use other techniques, as needed. In our example, the goal is to have no more than 125 silent auction packages valued from $123 to $160. We expect them to sell in the $80 range. An $80 sale seems to be a reasonable amount for someone to pay at a fundraiser, regardless of your location in the United States.

But there might be times where you determine you must sell each item for $500. Maybe that seems unlikely, given your crowd. Or maybe you have too many items, and your item count will be skewed. Maybe you have unusual items (nice, but unusual), and you know they aren't a fit for your guests.

There are many special situations, and it's impossible to cover them all here. Just know that an auction professional can offer ideas on making it all work. Options abound, and an expert can guide you.

Run your auction like a business.

After reading all these statistics, crunching the numbers, and perhaps running some calculations on your own silent auction results from last year, this might begin to feel a bit like analyzing a business.
Good!

The most important point I can share with you is to *run your auction like a business*. If all you glean from this chapter are those six words, it was worth your investment!

Let me share this story about a small benefit auction in a town a few hours from me.

In 2009, Leslie was perplexed. She'd volunteered to lead an auction, which, for the previous ten years, had consistently earned $17,000 to $19,000. Though the crowd was small (150 people), Leslie had a hard time believing the auction could only produce that much revenue.

She started educating herself.

First, she bought a book about benefit auctions and read it cover to cover. Then she went online and stumbled across my website. She saw I was speaking in a city about three hours away and decided to come. She and her best friend made a six-hour round-trip drive to participate.

On the way home, Leslie told her friend that everything she'd read and heard had convinced her that she needed to make some changes. Some of these changes would involve spending several thousand dollars. These were sizeable figures, given that this little auction had never raised more than $19,000.

Her best friend didn't know how to react. She knew Leslie would have a hard time convincing everyone to change. She wanted to be optimistic, but she sensed that few would support Leslie's decisions. Everyone's mind-set was that because the auction only made $17,000 to $19,000, it didn't make sense to *spend* money on it. After all, it didn't *make* that much.

But Leslie was adamant. Everything she'd learned indicated that change was necessary.

It wasn't easy; there was tremendous resistance. The committee refused to pay for some changes—like a professional benefit auctioneer. Undaunted, Leslie paid for those services herself. She just kept marching forward, implementing what she was learning.

The months rolled by, and finally, the auction date arrived. Not everything went as planned, but some things went better than expected. At the end of the night, when the totals were counted, the auction made almost $70,000. *It was $50,000 gain in one year.*

Mouths dropped. People screamed. Everyone was amazed. (And the committee reimbursed Leslie for the money she'd personally spent.)

Two years later, it came time to hold the next auction. No one wanted to plan the event. Everyone was convinced that the 2010 auction results would be impossible to replicate.

Again, Leslie stepped forward. At the end of the night, when the money was counted, the totals had risen. This time, more than $81,000 was raised.

Mouths dropped. People screamed. Everyone was amazed.

Because of poor auction management during the previous ten years, this event didn't realize it's potential. One might say that the event lost nearly $50,000 in each previous auction. The auction had been stuck making less than $20,000.

When Leslie assumed ownership, improvements followed. She became the CEO of her auction. She made hard decisions, and the auction improved.

Your auction is a business, and you are the CEO. As CEO, you have certain responsibilities, which include deciding on how you'll be improving this business.

In some ways, this leap of imagination shouldn't be difficult. You might already feel as if your auction is a retail store. You have opening and closing times. You have a variety of items to showcase and sell. You manage payments.

One substantial difference between your silent auction "store" and a retailer is that you have a limited amount of time to sell your merchandise. When a department store closes each night, they know they'll reopen the next morning, and the next morning, and the next. Some retailers are open every day of the year.

But your store is open a mere ninety to 120 minutes, *one day a year*. You lack the luxury of time. Because of this, you need to take a more aggressive approach to marketing and selling your items.

And just as the CEO of a company would weigh his options when it came to making financial investments, you'll do the same. Our end goal is to keep an eye on your yields so we can improve our net auction revenue.

Which reminds me of another story.

I was speaking in Pennsylvania a few years ago. As the participants introduced themselves, one woman said she hated to spend money on anything for the auction. "I know that everything I spend will take away from our bottom line," she wailed.

Well, she's wrong.

As we learned from Leslie's experience, some investments *make* you money.

CEOs make decisions every day. They must decide if they should buy *that* advertisement or *that* piece of software. They have to decide when to buy new computers, whether they can afford to make a cross-country trip to visit a customer, and whether to exhibit at a trade show. They must decide if it's worthwhile to buy a sponsorship to a charity auction like yours.

They can't afford to do *everything*, so they make decisions. They invest *here* and forgo *there* with an eye on growing the business.

Perhaps you've never run a business. If so, your silent auction will be your training ground. And as the CEO of your "auction business," you will start the process by deciding where you will *invest* money so you can *raise more* money.

"If I invest in *that*," you'll ask yourself, "will I raise substantially more money in my auction than if I *don't* buy it?"

To put it another way, you need to decide where you'll get the biggest bang for your buck. You might invest $5,000 and raise $20,000 more. Great! Or you might invest $5,000 and raise less. Ouch.

In Leslie's case, her largest expenditures were investing in a caterer, a professional auctioneer, and software. Your investments might be similar or different.

Don't be afraid to make a purchase if you believe it will help you raise more money. Auctions don't get big by playing small. Auctions get big when they start investing in the areas that will help them raise the most money.

Run your auction like a business.

The Three Legs of Your Gala

When I speak about gala auctions (whether silent or live), I share a visual of a three-legged stool. It's a visual to help us better understand how auction galas function and grow. If you've ever sat on a three-legged stool, you know that every leg supports your weight. You can comfortably sit on the stool, as long as all three legs are relatively the same length and girth. Even if you gained five hundred pounds, you could still sit on a three-legged stool, though the legs would have to be considerably thicker to accommodate your extra weight!

I liken auction galas to a three-legged stool. Each leg stands for a critical auction function and is necessary for your gala's success.

1. One of the legs is item procurement—or getting great items.
2. Another leg is audience development—or getting guests who have money to spend to attend your event.
3. The third is auction operations, which is a vast category covering everything from technology, checkout, time lines, décor, printing, marketing, and

more. It's a bit like the *behind the scenes* of an auction.

You need all three of these legs to be sturdy if they are going to support the ambitions of your gala. And just as the legs of a stool would need to be reinforced if you gained a significant amount of weight, the legs of the gala will need to become more robust as your event grows in size and complexity.

Auctions have many moving parts. In this chapter, we're limiting our scope to quick fixes that will improve your silent auction performance. That touches upon two of the three areas mentioned: item acquisition and auction operations.

New Places for Item Acquisition

The easiest and usually the best items are procured from people and businesses you already know. If you've run an auction for a while, you probably know that.

But here, I want to give you ten suggestions on where to get silent auction items your guests will love and your volunteers likely haven't considered.

1. **"Locally made" state websites**. Most states have a website for retailers who sell locally made products. In my home state of Kansas, it's www.KansasMadeProducts.com. California has www.MadeInCalifornia.net. Use the Internet to conduct a search, and see if a website is devoted to your state. Local producers are great potential donors. You might find a new source for fresh jams or clocks made of wheat husks.

2. **Google search for company +** *donation request.* As you shop for groceries, note the names of the companies whose products you purchased. When you get home, head to Google. Search for the name of that company and type *donation request*. From dog food to tissues, you'll be amazed at how many companies have standardized forms online for you to complete for auction donation requests.

3. **Book authors.** What's that book you've just downloaded into your Kindle? And what paperbacks did you take to the beach? Many popular authors have websites and donate a signed book or even sets of books to charities. Search for them online.

4. **Local cooking schools.** I bet you have a Julia Child or Rachael Ray wannabe attending your auction.

Local cooking schools often generously provide gift certificates for classes.

5. **Local tourist stores.** Visit your local tourism office, Convention and Visitors Bureau, AAA office, rental car agency, tourist hotel, or even a rest area along the highway. Depending on the location, you might find an entire case filled with maps and brochures from area vendors. Not only can you contact all of the companies who have a brochure, but note all of the companies advertising on the map itself. As you unfold the map, you'll see these companies with their advertisements wrapped around the sides of the map. Take note of the businesses that would most appeal to your crowd, and write them for a donation.

6. **Local malls.** Send your acquisitions team to the mall for the day. Common items my clients have received include reusable totes with the mall name, large paper bags (useful for auction checkout), promotional items, coupon books, coupons from stores, and even tickets to rides (some malls have rides such as carousels).

7. **A weekend vacation package.** Look at a map, and identify a few towns near you that could be a good weekend trip. Search on a travel website

(www.TripAdvisor.com is a good one), and see what businesses are listed when you search on that town. Start contacting those businesses. You might get a bed-and-breakfast to donate a night or two, a winery to donate a wine tour, a museum to donate admission tickets, and a restaurant to donate a gift card. Voila! With just a few e-mails, you've created a desirable weekend getaway.

8. **Kids' activities.** Sometimes Googling short phrases will reveal businesses to ask that you hadn't considered. For instance, *things to do in Baltimore with kids* will pull up some child-friendly activities. And by the way, try a different search engine. If you normally search on www.Google.com, try www.Bing.com or another search engine. Because of the way these companies chose to display search engine results, you can get different results on different search engines.

9. **Advertising/coupon packets, parenting catalogs, and magazines.** When you walk into your local businesses, notice the rack of free catalogs and magazines near the door. Pick up a few of those, and browse through for ideas. One of my clients saw an advertisement for a child's bounce

house and was able to get a rental donated. (No doubt it was used for a birthday party.)

10. **LivingSocial, Groupon, and other online coupon sites.** Consider joining an online coupon company (it's free) to monitor advertisers. Any business advertising such deep discounts through these sites is a good target for your donation letter.

Marketing Makeover to Improve Your Silent Auction Results

By now you've got the right number of items, packaged everything, and you're ready to start thinking about setting up your "auction store."

Good! Let's ensure your onsite marketing moves browsers into bidders. Here are five changes to fine-tune your silent auction yields. These often have the biggest impact on net income results to push you beyond that national average of 50%.

1: Use a sound system.

Perhaps the biggest misconception with a silent auction is the name. The name *silent auction* evolved because unlike a live auction (in which bids are cried by an auctioneer), a silent auction asks that bids be written onto a bid sheet (or punched into a device, like a mobile phone if an auction is using a mobile bidding system).

In that sense, the silent auction is silent because there is no auctioneer shouting numbers.

But too many planners seem to think it means that a silent auction can be ignored and still be successful. They think it can quietly sit over there, next to the wall, back in a corner, and guests will naturally seek it out and bid on items.

It doesn't work that way.

If you want guests to be engaged in the silent auction, you'll need to promote it. One of the best ways is to set up a sound system, and make announcements in your silent auction.

Just as retail businesses use sound systems to promote their specials, your auctioneer or emcee can use your sound system to advertise the silent auction, raffle tickets, and other activities.

When I was a child, Kmart advertised its blue light specials. "Attention, Kmart shoppers," we would hear. The announcer would then proceed to alert us to some great buy that was happening in one section of the store.

This type of promotion still happens today—because it works.

One Friday night, I was meandering through the deli department of my grocery store. I noticed the rotisserie chicken was on sale for $5. (It's regularly almost $9, so $5 was a good deal.) I put one in my cart.

As I started to push away, the deli manager picked up his phone and made an announcement heard throughout the store. "Attention, Safeway customers," he said. "Our nightly special is the rotisserie chicken for just $5. We only have four left in our deli department. Take dinner home tonight for just $5."

As I made my way around the aisle's end cap, I was almost trampled by a thirty-something guy running toward the deli to get one of those four remaining chickens!

That's an example of how a sound system sells products. Safeway didn't wait for customers to figure out that chickens were just $5 in the deli department. Safeway proactively *told* customers about the great deal and its limited quantity.

Your auctioneer or emcee needs to do the same. He should make announcements periodically. Maybe it's an announcement about the raffle tickets, which are selling rapidly and almost gone. Maybe it's about a special item.

"We've got a great trip to Orlando in our travel section," I might say. "It's just $500. Wow, you can spend a week with your family in Orlando for just $500. See Volunteer Sue here at the Travel Table. She'll show you where it is."

Your auctioneer should wander through the silent auction making these announcements.

2: Use lighting.
Let's put on our CEO caps and think like a business leader.

If you've got merchandise to sell, is your natural inclination to use dim lighting that makes the items difficult to see? Or install proper lighting so items are seen in their best light?

I know you selected the latter. It's common sense, isn't it? We want our customers (or bidders, in this case) to be able to see our items.

So why do so many silent auctions have horrible lighting? We invite our guests (many of whom are over the age of forty) to our store and then lower the lights. How can they see our merchandise in dim lighting?

Light is energy. Light is activity. Light is action.

Dim is quiet. Dim is low energy. Dim is, well, dim.

Two years ago, I started working with a new client. The silent auction area was beautifully arranged, and the committee had done an excellent job of showcasing items. As the sun set, the hallway became darker. It was becoming more and more difficult to see anything, especially the most expensive item—a $2,000 fur coat tucked into the corner.

As I stood there admiring the layout with the auction chair, she commented that it seemed to be getting dark. I agreed.

"What do you think about that?" she asked.

I said I was concerned. I knew that when the sun set, it would be too dark for the bidders to see easily. Although the hotel's wall sconces were illuminated, they didn't generate enough light to read bid sheets. In poor lighting, some bidders give up. They won't take the time to try and read. It can translate into lower sale prices.

The auction chair explained, "The gala chair thought that if we turned on the overhead lights, it might look like an eighth grade dance," she said. "She only wants the sconces on."

I turned to her with raised eyebrows and said, "Are we here to raise money, or are we here to foster a romantic environment?"

The auction chair took one look at me and marched off to find the hotel management. Within two minutes, the entire silent auction was flooded with lights, and it remained that way all night. (And by the way, that fur coat sold in the four figures!)

Your bidders with the most disposable income are typically over the age of forty. This is also the age at which most of us start to experience declining eyesight. If there's a question about whether the lighting will be adequate at your venue, consider enhancing ambient light with more direct light.

Not all venues will need extra lighting. If yours does, you can hire a professional lighting company to oversee it for you, or manage it in-house with a little planning.

Some of my clients ask volunteers to bring can lights and lamps from home. They position the lights to illuminate the tables. Another client searched online and found some inexpensive battery-operated lights. They measure just two-inch square and put out a strong beam. The client uses these every year, scattering them throughout the tables for extra light. Another client ingeniously used ball cap lights. The light has a clamp on the back that attaches to a ball cap's visor and shines down so the wearer can read a document. The auction décor committee took these lights and strategically attached them to displays to illuminate bid sheets.

3: Don't crowd items. Showcase them to sell for top dollar.

When you walk into a retail store, you can tell a lot about the value of the merchandise simply by observing how it's displayed.

Inexpensive items are often thrown into bins. At my office supply store, small bins filled with paper clips, erasers, and sticky notes are advertised with signs: "Any 3 items in these bins for $5.00!" When I visit discount stores, I see bins filled with underwear and socks: "Buy 5 pairs for $20." Post holiday sales in department stores have racks packed to the gills with clothing. The signs proclaim the deal: "Holiday closeout—75% off!"

In contrast, walk into a nice jewelry store and notice the difference.

The items are brilliantly showcased. The most expensive rings and necklaces are displayed with care, often in a case by themselves with no other jewelry to compete with their dazzle. A piece might be on its own pedestal with beautiful lights hitting the gem at all the right angles.

Retailers stack and pack cheap items. They throw them into bins. They tightly pack them onto shelves.

But when it comes to a valuable item for which they expect top dollar, that item is featured in an exquisite setting, by itself. The display screams, "I'm expensive and special."

Let's think about how this plays out in our auction because you, me, and all of our bidders have been conditioned by what we experience in these retail stores.

When we pack silent auction items onto tables, we broadcast a negative message. "This is a garage sale," we're subliminally conveying to guests. "We've got lots of cheap stuff on these tables. Don't pay much for any of it."

This is *not what we want to convey*!

Allow enough space to display items. A twelve-inch display would be a bare minimum for a display, and eighteen-inch to twenty-four-inch is more realistic. This translates into a standard eight-foot table accommodating about five items—three displayed on one side and two on the other.

Never have multiple rows of items on your tables. One of my clients had a standard eight-foot table with *three rows of items* displayed on it. It was too much merchandise for the area! Some guests avoided it entirely because it was too overwhelming.

Instead, plan extra space into your silent auction. Give your décor committee an adequate area to put out the bid sheet, a vertical description, and the item or a prop that represents and helps sell the item.

Once we have some space to spread out, this fourth marketing tip becomes easier to implement.

4: Use props.
At the clothing store, the retailer encourages us to try on the clothes before we buy them. At my favorite specialty grocer, they have fresh coffee available to drink. At the farmers' market, they hand out samples of seasonal fruit to lure me into buying.

That's part of the experience we want to create with our guests too. We create that experience by using props in our display.

Consider these examples:

- When a children's chorus sold three dozens of the executive director's "famous" chocolate chip cookies, they offered samples of the sweets right next to the platter that would be taken home by the winning bidder that night. It was a try-before-you-buy opportunity.
- A hospice client prepared three-ring binders of every vacation home being offered. Next to the bid sheet was a binder filled with photos of the home, the grounds, and spectacular views of the area.
- When a community foundation sold two tickets to the baseball game, they displayed it by showing a photo of the stadium with an *X* to mark the approximate seat locations. A bat was propped next to the bid sheet as well. They weren't *selling* the bat, but the display attracted bidders.

(If you're afraid someone will confusingly believe he/she is bidding on the prop, clarify by placing a small tent card next to it that reads, "For display only.")

Use props to sell the sizzle of each item. The bidder can begin to imagine owning the item.

5: Use guaranteed bid on silent auction bid sheets.
Our fifth improvement happens on the bid sheet (or in the mobile bidding device, should you happen to be using it).

It's called guaranteed bid, and it allows a guest to buy an item outright. If the guest agrees to the established price (set by you), he can immediately purchase the item. No more competing bids; the item is sold.

The set price is usually 150% of the value. So if your silent auction package is valued at $100, you'd set the guaranteed bid at $150. Your bidder would pay a "convenience fee" (if you want to think of it that way) of $50 to purchase the item.

On less popular items, you might price the guaranteed bid at 90% of value. On popular items, you might go as high as 200%.

Using this tool makes it easy for guests to buy. They don't have to wait around and monitor the bid sheet or their bidding device. This is one of the reasons we see men using this option more than women. Though some men like to shop, many would prefer to go into a store and buy what they want. It's a rare man who will dig around in his wallet to see if he happens to have a coupon, or who delays his purchase until the following week to see if the item goes on sale. Instead, men tend to buy it, be happy, and move on with their life. Guaranteed bid caters to them.

If you're using paper bid sheets (it doesn't work for mobile bidding), this technique also uses bidder psychology to attract bidders. When an item sells at the guaranteed bid price, your team will take a big marker and write SOLD! across the bid sheet. You might even choose to replace the bid sheet with a "SOLD AT THE GUARANTEED BID" sign. As guests browse your items, this serves as a visual reminder that items are being sold—*fast!* I've noticed that a "SOLD!" on a bid sheet will catch guests' eyes. They linger to see what they missed and then carefully start reading other items to see what's available.

Finally, guaranteed bid reduces the stress on your volunteers running checkout. If you're able to start selling some items earlier in the event, not so many items will pour into checkout at the same time. Your team can start to process sales earlier. It alleviates some of the pressure that will come later when the silent auction closes.

A Final Word

Profitable silent auctions are a blend of great items, a giving crowd, and effective back end processes. My clients have seen their auction returns improve (and hours of time saved) when they've incorporate the ideas shared here.

Though change isn't always easy, it can be worthwhile. If you see a great idea at your favorite retail business, think of how it can be incorporated into *your* business—*the auction*! Don't be afraid to experiment.

Additional Resources

- ***Fabulous Fund a Need Secrets: How to Double Your Benefit Auction Revenues in 15 Minutes***: http://www.redappleauctions.com/benefit-auction-webinars/fund-a-need-secrets/

- ***Rockin' Raffles for Auctions: How to Select, Structure, and Sell the Most Profitable Raffles for Your Gala for the Least Amount of Work***: http://www.redappleauctions.com/benefit-auction-webinars/raffles-for-auctions/

- ***Creative School Auction Themes, Centerpieces, and Décor: Simple to Sophisticated Designs, Ideas, and Activities That Make ANY Size Auction Memorable and Profitable***: http://www.redappleauctions.com/benefit-auction-webinars/School-Auction-Themes-Centerpieces-and-Decor

- **The Annual Auction Item Guide™**: http://www.redappleauctions.com/free-resources/benefit-auction-item-ideas-guide/

- ***Benefit Auction Ideas*** is an e-newsletter for auction planners sharing the inside scoop on planning an auction fundraiser: http://www.redappleauctions.com/free-resources/benefit-auction-ideas/

Chapter 9: Major Gift Fundraising
By Marc A. Pitman, CFCC

You've learned a lot in this book. Congratulations on making it this far!

In this chapter, you'll learn a way to take all you've learned so far and generate the most amount of cash for the lowest expense. You'll learn about asking people for money face-to-face!

Did you just freeze? Ask for money *in person?* Remind yourself to breathe. It will be okay. After I'm done showing you how, you may even find yourself enjoying it!

Does the thought of asking scare you to death?

Most people rank fear of asking for money before fear of untimely death. They'd rather die suddenly than ask people for money! Especially face-to-face. Sending a letter or an e-mail seems so much easier than actually facing a person. If this is you, you're in good company. For many of us, asking others for money is intimately wrapped up in our own views of money. Many of us were raised in families and faith traditions that didn't talk about money,

About Marc

Right out of college, I started working in the admissions office as an admissions counselor. One of the things I loved most about admissions was helping students identify their giftings and goals and see if our college was a good fit. But after a couple years, I hit a professional glass ceiling. There was no way for me to move up without moving to another college.

That's when I was approached by the development office. They told me that one of the benefits of development was getting to build relationships with donors in a similar way to the relationships I was building with prospective students. But where my admissions relationships had to start over every twelve months, donor relationships could be developed over many years.

That was appealing.

Within a few weeks, I was at my first ask. I was asking a donor to consider a gift of $100,000. Even though they didn't make the gift, I was hooked. I loved the process of lining up their values with the college's strategic objectives and trying to make a match.

I basically fell in love with asking.

Over the years, I started teaching others how I was approaching solicitations. I was shocked to discover that people told me they'd never heard these things taught the way I did. That I gave them a solid understanding of what to do and made it incredibly easy for them to actually do it.

As my career progressed to fundraising for a boarding school, then for arts organizations, a hospice, and rural hospitals, I learned a lot about setting up annual funds, planned giving programs, and special events. But major gifts and capital campaigns were the biggest part of my work. In all of it, I was able to coach hundreds of board members and volunteers. They told me that my approach to fundraising helped take the fear out of asking. With this newly found confidence, together we've raised millions and millions of dollars.

The coaching developed into creating The Fundraising Coach, a coaching and training firm, in 2003. I enjoy helping people fund their passion so much I started a free blog (FundraisingCoach.com) to share my systems with as many people as possible. Today it is one of the longest running blogs in the entire nonprofit sector.

After I'd been speaking and training for many years, some clients asked me to condense what I teach on asking into a book. Something that could be given to board members to help them get excited about asking, *and* to do that asking effectively. *Ask Without Fear!* was born! This book has sold around the world and been translated into multiple languages, helping organizations of all sizes with practical strategies to be fully funded.

I fell in love with fundraising about two decades ago, and I am still passionate about it! In fact, the only thing I enjoy more than asking people for money is coaching others to ask for money!

so naturally, we feel uncomfortable talking about it to others.

It's important to be aware of your own emotions around money. But your nonprofit needs you to get over it. So do the employees that will make their living in the nonprofit and especially the people it serves.

One of the most helpful acronyms for getting over fear is

FEAR =

> **False**
>
> **Evidence**
>
> **Appearing**
>
> **Real.**

That's often all fear is. Let's say you call a prospect, but they don't return the message. You could get all wrapped up in your head about it, creating a narrative that you must've annoyed them, and that you should never ask them. Or anyone else.

But that's just false evidence appearing real. In reality, they haven't returned your call. The rest of it is made up by your imagination.

What would happen if you harnessed that imagination for something positive? What if you imagined them, trying to get all their assets in a position to be able to significantly support you? Of them wanting to invest in your organization in a special way?

Sounds goofy or Pollyannaish. But it's just as made-up as the negative. And it puts you in a much better mind-set! The negative thinking is like an oppressive dark cloud hanging over your head. The positive outlook helps break up the cloud so you can get out there and raise money.

Simplicity builds confidence.

Fortunately, effective major gift fundraising is as easy as listening to people with a specific goal in mind. It's a conversation, not a monologue. And it's *not* listening to see when they are pausing so you can simply blurt out more information.

When I teach an overview of fundraising, I use the phrase *Get REAL.*

> **R**esearching your cause and your prospects.
> **E**ngaging your prospect.
> **A**sking. No one gives unless he/she is asked!
> **L**oving. Saying "thank you" is vital to ongoing successful fundraising.

These fit with everything you've read up to this point. But let's look at them a bit more in detail because each step of this process takes stress out of making a successful major gift solicitation.

Research

Research: Your Goal

I'm amazed at how few nonprofit people can tell me how much they need to raise. One successful nonprofit leader took *twenty minutes* to arrive at a number! How long would it take you? And "more" isn't an acceptable answer.

The first step of research is to find out how much money you need to raise. You started doing this as you read the chapters in this book on building your vision and telling compelling stories. One tried-and-true way nonprofits express their goal is in a document called a *case statement*.

A case statement is where you make the case for giving to your cause. You tell people why this is where they want to invest their hard-earned money. A good way to start this is by writing down all the things your nonprofit does. Throw in all the facts, figures, and statistics you can. But also put in the heartwarming stories. Don't just say that kids are helped; give real examples of kids. Tell their stories. Don't just say animals are better off when they're spayed or neutered; tell a story about what happens when they're not, and tell a story about what happens when they are. Not about the general animal population, but about one cat or dog. Don't just tell how many acres of land you've been able to put into conservation easements; tell the story of the people who have given those acres. Why did they go into this arrangement? How much more secure do they feel about the world they'll pass on to their kids and grandkids?

If you don't yet have a clear budget for the year, as you're putting this all in the case statement, keep a running tally of what each program will cost. Be sure to remember to include not only specific initiatives, but also the administrative or operating costs that will be required to make those initiatives possible.

When you have that large number, you'll be in a position to research how many gifts you'll need. If you're attempting to raise $100,000, the knee-jerk reaction will probably be, "We just need to find one hundred people who will give us $1,000." Don't. As nice as that seems, decades of fundraising experience show that that simply isn't how it works.

One of the most helpful tools for determining gift levels is a gift range calculator. A free online version can be found at www.GiftRangeCalculator.com. Calculators like this are based on the results of over seventy years of studying fundraising. This study shows that to successfully reach your fundraising goal, you'll need one gift to be 10–25% of your goal. The next should equal 7–15% of the total. The two after that should be 5–10% of your total, etc.

So to reach your goal of $100,000, you'll need at least one donor to give between $10,000 and $25,000. You'll also see on the gift range calculator that experience shows that you'll need to have four or five prospects to achieve each gift. Who are five people whom you think could give the $25,000 gift? And who are five people whom you think could give the $15,000? Who are ten people you think could give the two $10,000 gifts?

Research: Your Prospects

Working through the grid, you start building your prospect list. At the beginning, it's really more of a "suspect" list. These are people you suspect could give a gift. Part of the research step is to determine how many of these suspects can reasonably be called *prospects*—people you could reasonably sit down with and ask to invest in your cause.

You'll be amazed at how helpful Google is in this process. Simply searching on the person's name can bring up all sorts of helpful information. As can searching their name with the word *board* or *director*. Use this information, along with any your nonprofit might already have, to start building a profile of the prospect. Paid services like WealthEngine and NOZAsearch can help put your research on steroids. NOZA is a database of all publicly reported charitable giving. Just about any printed annual report finds its way into this database. Wealth Engine pulls publicly available information from all sorts of places, including stockholdings, property deeds, corporate and nonprofit board listings, charitable giving, airplane or yacht ownership, and more. It lists all this information in the form of a report. But more importantly, it uses a formula to help estimate the "gift capacity" for the person.

If your prospect runs a foundation in the United States, or *is* a foundation, GuideStar can be incredibly helpful. With only the free subscription, you can have access to their 990 reports. These IRS filings show how much income the foundation earned, how much it spent, who the key employees or board members are, and the specific grants they gave out in the year. This is particularly helpful if you were thinking of asking them for $25,000 but see that their top grants are consistently only $5,000. You can still ask for $25,000, but you'll now know you'll probably want to ask that as $5,000 a year for five years.

You need to take all this information with a grain of salt. It isn't flawless. But it is helpful in informing how you shape your approach to a prospect.

Your board members and a development committee can be a huge help in this research too. Whether you go over the list with them individually or create a formal peer review committee, you can benefit from their experience, knowledge, and connections.

One simple method of doing this is by conducting a "**CPI** screening"—rating each prospect on **Capacity**, **Philanthropy**, and **Interest.**

- Does the prospect have **CAPACITY**? Are they financially able to make a gift?
- Are they **PHILANTHROPIC**? Are they generous with their money? You need to be a good steward of your resources; if the prospect can't make a worthwhile gift or doesn't have a track record of giving, you would be better served seeking donations elsewhere.

- Are they **INTERESTED** in your cause? You can find this out by looking at other causes they've supported and by asking people close to your organization.

Have the people on the committee assign a score of 1 to 5 for each category—1 being lowest, 5 being highest. This tool can be useful because it removes individual personalities from the prospect rating process and makes it feel more objective. You should promptly visit anyone scoring 12 or more. But watch for those with high scores in the first two categories and some inclination to your cause. While you can't make someone wealthier or more generous, you *can* have a chance at making someone more interested in your organization. Which brings us to the second step: engage.

Engage

All this research can get a bit heady. You now know more about your prospects than you ever thought you would. You have even started creating specific strategies for your top prospects. But research alone will not raise money for your nonprofit. No money gets raised without someone being asked.

But jumping to the ask isn't the best strategy. Just as if you wouldn't propose marriage on a first date, you need to spend time to get to know your major gift prospect—and to let them get to know you. Like dating, major gift fundraising is about creating a relationship.

While the research helps you think you know about your donor, it really only gave you an outline, like the black lines in a coloring book. Engaging helps you color in the picture. There are all sorts of ways to engage your donor. Often, the first ask you make could be for them to come tour your location and see the great things happening. Or to come to an event. Or even to come have coffee with you.

One of the easiest ways you can remember to reach out to your top prospects is to set up Google Alerts. If you Google the word *alerts*, you'll find the link. This free service monitors news and blogs for whatever term or name you put in the search. When something happens, you get a notice and a link in your inbox. Simple. You should set up one for every top prospect. And one for each of your board members. As things come to your inbox, you can choose how to share that. If you read an article, you might print it out and scrawl a note across it, something like, "Great seeing you referenced here!" Or you could just bring it up in conversation when you see them next.

All of this is part of what most development professionals call "cultivation." This is where you plant and tend the seeds that your nonprofit will eventually harvest. Don't pull the plants up too soon. Even if the engaging just takes place over coffee before your ask, make sure your prospects know that they mean more to your organization than just being your checkbook.

Ask

The number 1 reason people don't give money to your cause is that they are not asked! So even if you skip the research and the engage steps, you'll raise some amount of money by consistently executing this one.

But if you've done the first two steps, this step will be quite fun. You'll already have the odds in your favor. You know what aspects of your nonprofit they are most likely to say yes to, and you'll have had time to shape the ask around their passions.

Preparing for the Appointment

When raising major gifts, it's always better to meet face-to-face. You can raise major gifts over the phone and in mail, but experience shows that people give more when asked in person.

Before you set up the appointment, be sure to have a specific dollar amount that you're planning on asking the prospect. Some fundraisers find it helpful to pull together a one- to two-page briefing with all the pertinent information that you know about the prospect. This could include:

- their name,
- name of their spouse/partner,
- their address,
- their past giving to your organization,
- other philanthropic giving they've done (that you could find),
- their bio (often from their business webpage or from notes in your database),
- a specific amount you hope they give, or
- any recognition that might be included at that gift level.

It can include just about anything that will help you make the ask. And it needs to be one or two pages.

Using a phone *is* a great way to set up the appointments. When you make the call, it's helpful to jot down two to three things you want to accomplish in the call, and keep those in front of you. They might be:

1. Smile.
2. Thank them for coming to the breakfast meeting.
3. Ask them for an appointment.
4. Get off as quickly as you can.

The call is just to set up an appointment, not to talk about the gift. Some people may outright ask you, "How much are you asking for?" It can be helpful to tell them that you have something to show them, or that this is important enough for you two to talk in person.

Any talk of gift amount at this stage will likely result in a reduced gift.

When making an appointment, I like to only ask for *twenty to thirty minutes* of their time. Twenty minutes is plenty and easier to fit in someone's schedule than forty-five. And if the prospect asks you questions that take longer than twenty minutes, it's his/her choice, not your fault.

I also prefer to not set these appointments at restaurants. If you have to, that's fine. But wait staff have an amazing ability to come to the table at exactly the wrong moment.

If you haven't been there yet, try having the meeting in a prospect's office or home. Seeing them in their "natural habitat" gives me clues about how to ask them. They may have lots of pictures of them shaking hands with famous people. They may have lots of plaques for their community service. Or they may have an understated office or home. Each of these might help you tweak the way you ask and will definitely give you cues on how to thank them when they make a gift.

Meeting in their office or home allows them to be in a place where they feel empowered and more at ease. Some fundraisers prefer to meet in a coffee shop or some other neutral ground—space where neither you nor they are in charge or are needing to save face. If you have that option, test to see if it works well for your asks.

One final thought on setting up the appointment: Tell them why you're coming. You probably won't want to say, "Hey, John. I want to hit you up for a major gift!" But you could say something more subtle like, "Hey, John. I'd love to meet with you for about twenty minutes to talk about the XYZ project we're doing here." Or, "Hi, Jane. I'd like to get together with you for twenty to thirty minutes to talk about your support of the ABC fund here."

That's enough to let them know yours is not simply a meet and greet. Sure, you'll still be cordial, but there is a purpose to your meeting.

At the Appointment

Being clear about the purpose of the appointment makes the appointment *so* much easier. If you've ever made an appointment using a phrase like "I'd just like to get together" when you really wanted to solicit the person, you know what I mean. In those meetings, you hardly hear the prospect. Your mental bandwidth is spent trying to twist what the prospect is saying to fit the sales pitch you feel you need to deliver!

But with the more specific approach advocated here, the appointment is, in many ways, more relaxed. You have a strategy for why you think this prospect would be interested in making a significant investment in your nonprofit. And your intentionality in setting up the appointment makes it so that even if you get lost in chitchat, the prospect will bring the conversation around to the ask.

On your way over to the meeting, keep practicing the ask. "I'd like to ask you to consider a gift of $150,000 to this fund." "Would you consider a gift of $150,000 to the campaign?" Even, "I have *no* idea what to ask you. Would a gift of $150,000 be something you'd consider?"

An ask isn't an ask unless you mention a specific dollar amount. Anything else is a cop-out. "Would you consider supporting this?" doesn't let your prospect know what you were thinking. You might want $25,000, but they might only give $250 because they are supporting you. So respect them enough to get the full dollar amount. And practice that line over and over on your way over. The more you practice the dollar amount, the smoother it will come out at the solicitation.

When you get to the meeting, feel free to take a drink or cookie if they offer. Water is usually always appropriate. You might comment on their office or home or one to two things in there. You could ask them what they like about the organization. Or what they like most about what they've learned. Remind yourself to be truly interested.

But remember, you only asked for twenty minutes. So honor that by getting to the ask. You might pull out a copy of the gift range calculator you used to figure out funding levels. This shows them that you have a plan, and that you're not asking them to be the sole funder. Then you can say, "You know, Joe, you mentioned your love for blue vases. We're expanding our collection. Would you consider a gift of $150,000 to help us expand our blue vase collection?"

Then, SHUT UP!

Sales trainers say, "He who speaks next loses." That isn't the case here. Fundraising isn't a win/lose situation. But think of it from the donor's perspective. You've just asked them to do something they may never have done. At least not at that level. So you need to respect them enough to give them as much space to process as they need.

Sit calmly. Take a sip of coffee or water. But try not to move too much, and *definitely* do not speak.

The prospect needs to think how they'll make the gift. Do they have that kind of money in the bank? How will they explain it to their business partner? How will they explain it to their spouse?

They have a lot to consider. And they'll let you know they're done by being the first to speak.

This is the hardest time for fundraisers. This silence feels like a free fall—you are completely out of control. Everything in you is screaming to say something. ANYTHING! But resist that urge and let them process.

The ability to be silent after an ask is the difference between solvent nonprofits and failing nonprofits.

Learn to be comfortable with silence.

When They Next Speak

When they finally speak (it'll probably be far shorter than you feel it was), there are three possible outcomes.

1. **They'll say yes.**

   Congratulations! Now you can whip out a pledge form and have them sign it! If they say yes really quickly, you either did great research, or you asked for too little. If they whip out a checkbook, you might try calmly saying, "A year for the next three years?" If you can pull this off naturally, you may be able to increase their gift. If not, no worries.

2. **They'll say no.**

It's rare at this stage in the process to get an outright no. You've usually weeded those out in the research and engage steps.

3. **Or they'll come up with objections.**

An objection may sound like a no with a rational argument to back it up.

A major gift ask is only as effective as the close. If you ask, but the person doesn't make a decision, you may feel good for asking, but your nonprofit still has no money. The most basic way to close the ask normally looks like answering objections. The person didn't say yes right away. But they didn't say no either. Instead, they thought of reasons they couldn't give. These are objections. And these are completely normal.

Objections are great. They let you keep a conversation going. In making an ask, you've put the prospect on the spot. Helping with objections allows you to show them that you are, figuratively, on the same side of the table. You need to hear each objection as a request. The prospect might say, "I'm sorry, my kids are in college right now." But you need to hear, "My kids are in college right now. Can you help me figure out how I can make such a large gift and still make tuition payments?" The more you see objections as requests for help, the easier it will be for you to work through this phase.

Your researching your cause will help here. You'll have the facts and figures to clear up misconceptions that they have. You'll have stories you can point to as a form of proof that your cause works.

This is where options like monthly giving or multiyear pledging can be helpful too. I love multiyear pledges. This gives you much more time to be able to thank a donor. Some people recommend leading the ask with options like this. Instead of asking for $7,500, they suggest asking for $2,500 a year for the next three years. I prefer the full dollar amount for two reasons. First, it gives the prospect more of a deer-in-the-headlights response. "Wow. She is asking me to make her nonprofit a priority." Second, most of us aren't that great doing verbal math problems. You may lose the prospect as she tries to figure out what $2,500 a year for three years adds up to. But this is more a personal preference than hard-and-fast rule.

If you've been in this stage of the asking process before, you know some prospects are amazing objection generators! They seem to have an endless well of excuses and reasons they can't give. You have to remember that *your job is not to have an answer for every objection.* Your job is to raise money. Here are two great responses to help you get off the objection treadmill.

The first treadmill-busting phrase is:
"That is another great question. Let me ask you, if I can answer this to your satisfaction, is this the last thing standing in the way of your making the gift?"

If it's not, they'll let you know! They may be talking about budget allocations, but they're really upset about something your CEO did. This gives them a chance to dig up the real grievance and gives you the chance to only focus on the objections that matter.

The second treadmill-busting phrase is:
"That is interesting. If I can't answer this to your satisfaction, does that mean you wouldn't make the gift?"

I love this one. Again, you're stopping the objections and asking if this is a deal breaker. You'll be surprised how often a prospect will say, "You know, it won't. I would like to make that gift."

Both of these are called "test closes." They are testing to see if the prospect is ready to give. And both of these work.

Leaving the Appointment

It's best to leave the appointment with a signed pledge. Something in writing saying how much the donor intends to donate. But this isn't always possible. If the prospect needs to think it over, or ask a spouse, make sure to get a time to talk with them. "If I haven't heard from you before Thursday, may I give you a call?"

Getting this type of permission makes following up so much easier. Without this permission, you'll be consistently wondering if you're bugging the person or following up too soon. With the permission, you've both agreed on a follow-up time.

LOVE

I originally called this step Live/Like/Love. Because some of the times, it will be easy to show love to prospects. But sometimes you'll have to choose to like their decision. And at times, you'll have to learn to simply live with the outcome.

If the prospect says yes when you've asked, you simply need to be sure to thank them about seven times before you ask them again. A gift acknowledgment within twenty-four to forty-eight hours is standard. A personal note from you after the meeting is terrific. And then your nonprofit should have systems for who else (development director, executive director, board chair) writes notes or makes calls. This is often based on the size of the commitment, but it can be based on the person too.

This is also another place where your research and engaging pays off. You'll have a good sense whether they'd like to be publicly recognized in a splashy way or just quietly have tea with the CEO.

But fundraising is all about relationships. The work really starts if they've said no. The big thing is to not burn any bridges. If you made it all the way to the ask, you had good reason to believe they'd say yes. The timing simply might not have been right. If you keep in touch with them, they just may give in the future. People will remember you if you're exceptional at handling a no. And refusing a request can be so difficult they may be grateful for your ability to take their refusal well. A no now is rarely a no forever.

One way of thanking donors can be by making certain gift ranges into giving clubs like The President's Circle or some such thing. Another could be attaching naming opportunities to certain gift levels. It can also be helpful to break your goals into nameable chunks and projects like the Joe CEO Honorary Training or the Big Corporate Airlines Institute. You might be able to use those to pitch to people that their names will be in the press releases and other publicity. This would be wonderful for your nonprofit *and* give the sponsor visibility as well.

Gift ranges, naming opportunities, and sponsorship levels can be extremely effective ways to "tangibilitize" giving, to help donors feel as if they're giving something concrete. If you haven't yet, check out http://heifer.org/ to see how they make giving tangible. Be sure to check out the small print too. They're very clear that every gift is a gift to Heifer Project's mission, not necessarily to the goat or chickens you're "buying."

Whatever you do to say "thank you," remember: People are always worth far more than the amount of money they can give you. So treat them well.

The Two Basic Groups of Major Gift Donors

Now you're ready to start asking. There are two groups for you to ask from: those who already know you and those who don't.

Those Who Know You

Those who know you are probably already enthralled with what you're doing. Ask them for money! Especially the board members. Major donors and foundations may well ask what percent of the board is giving to the project. Note: Not *how much* the board is giving, but *how many* of the board are giving. 100% board participation is the goal. If the whole board *isn't* giving, it'll probably jeopardize your fundraising effectiveness.

Steps:

1. Make a list of all those who know about your initiative.
2. Run them through a quick CPI screening, more to determine whether you want to ask them for a certain amount or simply for a "participation gift."
3. Ask them.
4. Be sure to show them how their gift is changing the world.

Those Who Don't Know You

Because this group is so big, it would be *very* easy to get unfocused. Always follow up every solicitation with something like, "Do you know other people that may be interested in learning about what we're doing?" You may yield names from such a simple question.

Here is a plan for asking for gifts from people you don't know (in this case, corporations):

1. Make a list of people and companies. Start with ones that you suspect have capacity, are philanthropic, and/or interested. As you pursue these leads, you may become aware of companies or people that just

seem to be overwhelmingly generous. They may be worth adding to your list.

2. Since these will be mostly cold calls, do a quick check of the website to get:

- An overall feel for how this company communicates. (Is it formal and traditional or cutting-edge and informal?)
- What their mission statement or values are.
- The name of the VP of marketing (you may have to call for this). Always go to the marketing department first. Even if the company is progressive enough to have a charitable office, marketing will *always* have the bigger budget.
- The company's e-mail protocol (firstname_lastname? firstinitiallastname? etc.). This could help you break through the gatekeepers and communicate with the VP directly.

Making the ask.

- Based on your quick survey, determine what level or naming opportunity you intend to ask them for. You may only have thirty to sixty seconds to make the ask. Make it specific. How will this help the company or individual? How will it help your nonprofit?

- Explain who you represent, why you're calling (what leads you to believe it may interest them), and what you're asking for quickly and succinctly. They don't have time for normal calls, let alone cold calls!

This may sound simple, and it should. But it'll take lots of work to get it done. I hope you see how this simple process can be morphed to fit approaching individuals and foundations. If you're asking foundations, be sure to follow their specific format for asking. Those guidelines are usually available on their websites.

Remember, every year more than $200 billion is given to nonprofits in the USA alone. Your nonprofit could definitely get a piece of those philanthropic dollars. But you need a realistic goal, a compelling story, and a disciplined approach to fundraising.

Congratulations! You're embarking on a wonderful adventure; I'm convinced asking people for money is one of the best vocations in the world!

Additional Resources:

- ***Ask Without Fear!*** (book and DVD):
  http://fundraisingcoach.com/ask-without-fear/

- ***Fundraising Kick*** (weekly coaching e-mails):
  http://fundraisingcoach.com/fundraisingkick/

- **The free *Ask Without Fear!*** e-mail newsletter:
  http://fundraisingcoach.com/subscribe/

- ***Who's Telling Your Story?*** (book and webinar):
  http://fundraisingcoach.com/storytelling/

- ***Nonprofit Social Media: A Beginner's Guide***:
  http://fundraisingcoach.com/nonprofit-social-media/

About the Authors

Betsy Baker

Betsy Baker is president of YourGrantAuthority.com. She has a master's in Public Administration from Auburn University and is an author, trainer/coach, and public speaker. She has raised more than $10 million in grant funding. Betsy is a regular presenter for the Foundation Center, the Grant Professionals Association, the Georgia Center for Nonprofits, and United Way agencies, and is a regular contributor to Opportunity Knocks!, CharityHowTo, and CharityChannel. She also hosts her own webinars and workshops through her website. For **a free grant assessment rating system**, register at: http://yourgrantauthority.com/grant-sat/#.

Kirsten Bullock, CFRE, MBA

Kirsten Bullock, CFRE, MBA, is the founder of TheNonprofitAcademy.com. She works with entrepreneurial nonprofit leaders to help them involve more people in their organizations and raise the money they need. She earned her designation as a certified fundraising executive in 2002.

Since 1995, Kirsten has worked with health care organizations, social service providers, national and local ministries, and international membership associations. These have included organizations such as AIDS Interfaith Ministries of Kentuckiana, Presbyterian Women National Offices, Community Health Centers, Inc., and the Institute of Internal Auditors Research Foundation.

Kirsten is currently serving as immediate past president of the Association for Fundraising Professionals–Greater Louisville Chapter. She is an AFP master trainer and has presented for the Indiana Library Federation, Business First (Louisville), Kairos Prison Ministry International, Steward's Staff, and Boys and Girls Clubs of America. In addition, she compiles *Kirsten's Fundraising Headlines Blog*, is the author of *Simple Steps to Growing Your Donors,* and runs TheNonprofitAcademy.com.

Kirsten is a licensed fundraising consultant in Kentucky. She holds a bachelor's degree in Social Work and a master's of Business Administration. When not working to equip and empower people in the nonprofit sector, Kirsten sculpts, is attempting to learn to speak Danish, and enjoys living in the Highlands in Louisville, Kentucky, with her husband, Rob.

Gayle L. Gifford, ACFRE

Gayle L. Gifford, ACFRE, is president of Cause and Effect, Inc., a consulting firm that helps nonprofits build their capacity for greater impact. Gayle's expertise includes governance, strategic and business planning, organization and fund development, and public engagement design. Gayle is one of only one hundred individuals in the United States to have earned the advanced fundraising credential ACFRE.

A nationally known writer and presenter, Gayle is author of *How to Make Your Board Dramatically More Effective, Starting Today*, and a contributor to three other books on nonprofits published by CharityChannel Press. Gayle is an adjunct instructor in the master's program in Public Humanities and Cultural Studies at Brown University. Prior to starting Cause & Effect, Gayle served in senior management, fundraising, and communications roles at PLAN International USA, Save the Bay, and City Year RI. Gayle holds an MS in Organization and Management from Antioch University–New England and a BA in Geography from Clark University.

In addition to her service on the WaterFire Providence board of directors, Gayle serves on the board of Blackstone Academy Charter School and on the advisory councils of Latino Dollars for Scholars and Rhode Island Museum of Science and Art. Gayle has three great adult children, a wonderful husband and business partner, Jonathan W. Howard, and is proud to live in one of the most vibrant cultural cities in the USA—Providence, RI.

Pamela Grow

Author, coach, copywriter, and nonprofit marketing consultant, Pamela is publisher of *The Grow Report*, the leading free weekly e-zine for small shop fundraisers. She's also the author of *Five Days to Foundation Grants*, the first online grant-writing guide, and the creator of *Simple Development Systems Members*, providing donor-focused fundraising and development training for small nonprofits.

In 2010, Pamela was named one of the 50 Most Influential Fundraisers by *Civil Society* magazine; and in 2013, she was named one of the Top 40 Most Effective Fundraising Consultants by the *Michael Chatman Giving Show*. She's been featured by the Chronicle of Philanthropy and the Foundation Center and cohosts *Little Shop*, a regular column of *Fundraising Success* magazine. She is a regular contributor to SOFII, the showcase of fundraising innovation and inspiration, and CharityChannel. Pamela has presented at the annual Nonprofit Technology Conference , the New Jersey Association for Grant Professionals, and Network for Good's 911 webinars. She hosts regular grant-training webinars with CharityHowTo.

Pam segued from six years working in programming and communications at a regional grantmaking foundation to the world of fundraising ten years ago. In her first position as a fifteen-hour-a-week development director for an agency with a $3 million dollar budget, she increased individual giving by 25%—while reducing costs by 31%—and increased foundation funding by an astonishing 93%!

Committed to empowering small shop fundraisers everywhere with the tools for sustainable funding, Pamela has collaborated on fundraising systems like *100 Donors in 90 Days*, the *Donor Retention Project*, and the upcoming *Better Boards in 90 Days*. In her spare time, Pamela is a Food Network junkie and bakes a killer strawberry rhubarb pie, paints, runs, lifts weights, practices yoga, and is a single mother to two utterly remarkable daughters.

Lori L. Jacobwith

Lori L. Jacobwith has a passion for the positive. Her strategies and tools have helped organizations to collectively raise more than $200 million from individual donors over the past decade. She has coached and trained thousands across North America to raise more money and powerfully share their stories.

Lori is the founder of the *Ignited Online Fundraising Community*,[13] the author of *Nine Steps to a Successful Fundraising Campaign*[14] and author of the must-read fundraising coaching blog *Withism's From Lori: Boldness, Clarity and Wisdom for Fundraising Professionals.*[15]

In 2013, Lori created the *Imagine What's Possible Step-by-Step Storytelling System*[16] for nonprofits who want to raise more money from individual donors with ease.

Lori lives in Minnesota and is a longtime member of the Association of Fundraising Professionals [AFP]. You can learn more about Lori at www.lorijacobwith.com. Follow Lori on Twitter (@ljacobwith), or get daily coaching tips from Lori on Facebook (LJacobwith).

---

[13] http://www.lorijacobwith.com/membership
[14] http://www.lorijacobwith.com/free-resources
[15] http://www.lorijacobwith.com/store/withisms-from-lori-boldness-clarity-wisdom-for-fundraising-professionals-making-a-difference
[16] http://www.lorijacobwith.com/storytellingsystem

Marc A. Pitman, CFCC

An international nonprofit organizational development consultant and fundraising trainer, Marc A. Pitman helps nonprofit board members get excited about asking for money. He is the author of *Ask Without Fear!*[17] and founder of *FundraisingCoach.com*, a website dedicated to practical ideas for fundraising more effectively.

Because of his dynamic trainings, Marc speaks to thousands each year at events like the World Fundraising Summit in Mexico, Association for Fundraising Professionals International Conference, and organizations around the world. His experience in nonprofit fundraising and leadership training has caused him to be featured in books and articles and be sought out as a guest on TV and radio shows as diverse as Al Jazeera and Fox News.

Committed to making it ridiculously easy for board members, volunteers, and nonprofit staff to get fundraising training, Marc continues to write books, create fundraising training DVDs, and collaborate on systems like *100 Donors in 90 Days*.

Marc's experience also includes planting and pastoring a Vineyard church, managing a gubernatorial campaign, teaching Internet marketing at both the undergraduate and graduate level, and being chosen as one of Maine's first 40 Under Forty, honoring Maine's emerging generation of leaders.

He is the husband of his best friend and the father of three amazing kids. And if you see him drive by, he'll probably be singing '80s tunes loud enough to embarrass his family.

---

[17] fundraisingcoach.com/ask-without-fear/

Sherry Truhlar

Benefit auctioneer Sherry Truhlar escaped a corporate cubicle to launch Red Apple Auctions.

Today she works as a charity auction educator and onstage auctioneer, helping schools and nonprofits across the USA plan more profitable benefit auctions. Her galas have raised $15,000 to $2 million each, and she's sold at events with crowds up to 1,200.

A prolific writer for her own blog and other fundraising sites, her advice is tapped by thousands of auction planners seeking to improve their benefit auctions. She's been covered in *Town & Country* magazine, *The Washington Post Magazine*, *Auctioneer*, and other publications.

As auctioneer, Sherry has an elegant presence and warm persona, which elevates the live auction at many galas. At almost six feet tall, she commands the stage and comfortably connects with male and female guests.

An avid self-educator, she holds many educational credentials. She is thought to be the only auctioneer who has achieved a Certified Meeting Professional (CMP) designation and is also a graduate of the Certified Auctioneers Institute (CAI). She holds a professional certificate in event management from George Washington University, the Benefit Auctioneer Specialist (BAS) designation from the National Auctioneers Association, an MA degree from the University of Wollongong (Australia), and BA and BS degrees from Emporia State University.

Sandy Rees, CFRE

Sandy Rees CFRE, creator of the GetFullyFunded system, helps nonprofit leaders raise the money of their dreams and build successful boards. She's a coach and consultant and provides clients with the how-to of fundraising as well as helps with personal/professional development.

Sandy is the author of *Get Fully Funded: How to Raise the Money of Your Dreams, 6 Figure Fundraising, Fundraising Buffet,* and *Simple Success Fundraising Plan.* She's a frequent contributor to *Fundraising Success* magazine and authors the blog *Get Fully Funded.*

Sandy is an accomplished presenter and an AFP master trainer. She's led fundraising seminars for the Association of Fundraising Professionals, the Chattanooga Center for Nonprofits, and many local, regional, national, and international conferences.

Sandy lives with her family on a small farm in Loudon, TN.

Contact info:

Phone: 865-216-0083
E-mail: sandy@sandyrees.com

Websites:
www.sandyrees.com
www.getfullyfundedblog.com
www.deadlyfundraisingmistakes.com

Resources from The Nonprofit Academy:

Companion Worksheets for The Essential Fundraising Handbook for Small Nonprofits
These worksheets have been resized to be easily printed out and used in your day-to-day work. They include worksheets from the book as well as a few additional resources (such as a personal board member fundraising plan and a sample prospect profile form):
http://thenonprofitacademy.com/handbook-worksheets/

Fundraising Planning Worksheets
These worksheets were designed as a supplement to the fundraising planning chapter in *Simple Steps to Growing Your Donors* by Kirsten Bullock. They are helpful as a standalone guide or in conjunction with the book:
http://thenonprofitacademy.com/free-worksheets/

CPSIA information can be obtained
at www.ICGtesting.com
Printed in the USA
LVOW10s1613190417

531397LV00009B/865/P